THE NAKED ENTREPRENEUR

THE NAKED
ENTREPRENEUR

DAVID ROBINSON

**KOGAN
PAGE**

Acknowledgements

I am very grateful to numerous clients, friends and colleagues who have contributed, in different ways, to the material which I used in writing this book. I particularly wish to acknowledge the help of Professor Michael Earle for allowing me access to the library of Templeton College, Oxford, to the staff of the Information Department of Spicer & Oppenheim and to a number of secretaries at my firm who worked tirelessly on the preparation of the text.

First published in Great Britain in 1990 by Kogan Page Limited, 120 Pentonville Road, London N1 9JN.

British Library Cataloguing in Publication Data
A CIP record for this book is available from the British Library.

ISBN 0-7494-0084-6
0-7494-0003-X Pbk

Typeset by The Castlefield Press Ltd., Wellingborough, Northants.
Printed and bound in Great Britain by Richard Clay,
The Chaucer Press, Bungay

Contents

Chapter 1

Introduction

A matter of definition

If you are walking down a street with a friend and he points to someone and says, 'That's John – he's an entrepreneur', what sort of person do you imagine? Is John the local bingo hall baron or property magnate? Is he a bond dealer at some merchant bank or the owner of the video store in the high street? Does he drive a Porsche and have a villa in Portugal, or have two children at public school and life membership of the local golf club?

Any, or all, of these descriptions could be true. The word 'entrepreneur' is increasing in everyday use in the vocabulary of our enterprise society. Literally, it means someone who 'carries something between' two parties – in other words a middleman. But an entrepreneur is not an altruistic or disinterested party: quite the contrary – he is distinctly interested in profit and wealth creation.

Middlemen come in all shapes and sizes but the implicit assumption is that they actually do little real work. The middleman is thought of as a 'smart aleck' who makes a profit at the expense of two, less bright, colleagues. By this definition, the entrepreneur would do little to create wealth – just siphon off some for himself. However, this is far from real life observation of the entrepreneur.

Few entrepreneurs, if any, could be described in these crude and simplistic terms. The character we are seeking to define is much more complex and elusive than this literal extension of the word would suggest. More recognisable, perhaps, is the picture of the entrepreneur as 'super hero' – the wealthy, larger than life risk-taker and business autocrat. He may be tinged with megalomania, and his activities admired and written about alongside those of pop stars and politicians. Living in a world apart from ordinary mortals, such people seem to have the power to change the destinies not only of companies but of whole industries.

This archetype too is inadequate. There are very few who fit this mould and they are scarcely representative of what is acknowledged as a large and growing group of people both in the UK and internationally.

For the purposes of this book, we need a recognisable set of assumptions about the sort of person we are examining. No definition can be either comprehensive or wholly satisfactory: all that can be aimed for is a sufficiently wide scope for *most* of the target group to be included.

We shall assume that our 'entrepreneur' is:

- involved in what may generally be described as 'business', whether making, selling or trading in things;
- the sole proprietor of his or her enterprise – although, as we shall discuss later, entrepreneurial partnerships offer an interesting exception to this assumption; and
- established in the sense of having satisfied his immediate material needs but remaining ambitious to grow in influence and wealth.

These assumptions describe entrepreneurs in terms of what they do and how they do it.

An alternative description can be based not on what they *do* but on what they *are*. The contention of this book is that you can just as certainly recognise an entrepreneur from the way he or she thinks and behaves as from whether he has made a million or ten million pounds. It argues that within a broad section of people drawn from widely differing backgrounds, cultures and intellectual groups some key traits are commonly discernible. Many years' experience suggest that they occur with sufficient frequency to offer some general insights which may prove useful both to the independent observer and to the entrepreneur himself. (For simplicity the personal pronoun 'he' is used throughout the text to include both the male and female genders.)

Our aim is to strip away the hyperbole and self-promotion and explore the characteristics which go into the make-up of the entrepreneur, relying on the findings of academics, the revelations of individuals in their more unguarded and frank moments of self-analysis; but, most of all, on 25 years' experience of close personal and working relationships with entrepreneurs – both the successful and the failures. Observing the 'naked' entrepreneur is not a voyeuristic and destructive process – it is an instructive one. It will help us to understand some of those inner motives which contribute to the energy and commitment that single out the entrepreneur from his fellow men. It will help us to recognise the early indications of entrepreneurial capacity and to encourage and nurture them. It will also warn us of the dangers of making invalid assumptions about how such individuals are likely to behave in particular circumstances. Most of all, it aims to offer some new insight into the behaviour of a group of people whose activities are of fundamental importance to the growth of any free enterprise economy.

In summary, then, an entrepreneur, whether male or female, has already chosen a way of life dedicated to the pursuit of money and power, has demonstrated some success in that pursuit and shown business associates, staff, friends and family those qualities (both endearing and less so!) which have contributed to that success.

Born or made?

The point of departure on our journey of exploration must be to seek some answer to the question of whether the entrepreneur springs from the cradle with all his faculties, drives and traits preformed, needing only the opportunity to exploit them later in some suitable business environment; or whether the entrepreneurial character is formed by a process of 'conditioning', by a combination of circumstances and the example (and influence) of others.

This question is important for a number of reasons. If entrepreneurs are 'born', then once we can identify and understand the main distinguishing characteristics, there is little point in those lacking them to attempt to embark on such a path: the likelihood of failure would be too great. Equally, those responsible for developing an individual's talents, whether school teachers, trainers or business superiors, would be advised to concentrate on more useful skills than encouraging independent enterprise. If it was certain that these distinguishing features were 'born' into individuals, this would equally suggest that talent spotting for the budding entrepreneur would, indeed, start in the school playground.

Conversely, proof of the proposition that entrepreneurs are 'made' by their experiences and working environment would encourage the creation of such conditions, particularly within established businesses. Many companies have attempted to establish a 'nursery' for budding entrepreneurs – generally, it must be said, with poor results.

The answer to this question lies in what John G Burch, writing in the September–October 1986 edition of *Business Horizons* calls 'the galaxy of personality traits (which) characterise individuals who have a propensity to behave entrepreneurially'. He lists nine as being 'more salient'. These are:

1. *A desire to achieve* – the push to conquer problems and give birth to a successful venture.
2. *Hard work* Most entrepreneurs are workaholics (in many instances they have to be in order to achieve their goals).
3. *Nurturing quality* They take charge of and watch over a venture until it can stand alone.
4. *Acceptance of responsibility* They are morally, legally and mentally accountable for their ventures.
5. *Reward orientation* They want to achieve, work hard and take responsibility, but they also want to be rewarded handsomely for their efforts – and rewards can come in forms other than money, such as recognition and respect.
6. *Optimism* They live by the philosophy that this is the best of times and that anything is possible.
7. *Orientation to excellence* They often desire to achieve something outstanding that they can be proud of – something first class.
8. *Organisation* Most are good at bringing together the components of a venture – they are wholly 'take charge' people.
9. *Profit orientation* They want to make a profit, but the profit serves primarily as a meter to gauge their degree of achievement and performance.

Of these traits, two stand out as being more likely to be 'inborn' qualities than the others – the desire to achieve and the capacity for hard work. Several research studies have shown that entrepreneurs are convinced that they can command their own destinies. In the jargon of the behavioural scientist, the 'locus of control' of the entrepreneur lies within himself rather than the world about him. He believes that his destiny lies in his own hands rather than as a consequence of the actions of others. While this is also a fairly common characteristic of successful leaders, whether in business or not, it exists in such a sharply emphasised form in the entrepreneur that it can verge on the obsessive. It is this self-belief which stimulates him to act in a highly individualistic and often rebellious way. It creates an attitude which accepts amounts of work which would be quite unacceptable to ordinary mortals, encourages persistence long after others have given up and underpins a reputation for unswerving dedication to a concept, product or business initiative.

The capacity to work exceptionally hard (and long) in pursuit of a particular project requires a combination of physical, emotional and intellectual energy which cannot be artificially stimulated – except in short bursts. We are all familiar with the adrenalin surge which accompanies the achievement of an exceptional task. Feats of endurance and resilience are almost as commonplace on the battlefields of commerce as they are in those of real wars. The extraordinary facility of the entrepreneur is to sustain that same commitment and capacity *in the long term*. Entrepreneurs claim that the 'work' involved is almost wholly pleasurable and that their unstinting commitment to it is therefore no more than self-indulgence. This may be true from their point of view. Those working with the entrepreneur, exhausted from trying to keep pace with the unbounding energy he shows, would equally argue that the effort involved is 'work' of a very demanding order. They would leave us in no doubt that this characteristic is both exceptional and rare.

While a facility to organise, to understand and manage risk, and to be strongly motivated by personal gain, can be developed in individuals in the appropriate environment, it seems that these two, basic character traits must be inborn if the entrepreneur is to succeed. Writing about their early lives (normally with an eye to making the best of the story), many successful businessmen reflect on how they exploited their first opportunity. It seldom seems to have been either an easy or an uncomplicated breakthrough. In every case, there was a moment of truth – a point of decision when a 'safe' option was rejected and a risk undertaken. Was it a calm, cold and rational decision or impulsive and intuitive? Whatever intellectual processes were at work it seems certain that the 'demon' driving the entrepreneur took hold at that moment and a career was launched.

How entrepreneurial are you?

John Burch offers a further insight into the 'tendencies' which indicate how entrepreneurial (or non-entrepreneurial) individuals are likely to be. His matrix is reproduced opposite.

At the 'non-entrepreneurial' end of each axis is the person least likely to take that role – in Mr Burch's analysis, a labourer. At the other end is the person most likely to take that role – what he calls the 'inventrepreneur' – who not only exploits an idea but invents it in the first place! Between these two extremes he shows examples of the types of job people may have, corresponding to the 'tendencies' they show.

In common with most models, this matrix contains elements of both simplification and generalisation. Although it should, for this reason, be approached with some caution, it does offer an interesting, if rather rudimentary, basis for self-assessment. If your personal behaviour is firmly at the right-hand end of the scale for *all elements*, you have the makings of an entrepreneur. If any veer to the left of the centre line, however marginally, think again!

A structured approach

Research into entrepreneurial behaviour is concentrated on three, archetypal roles as:

- innovator
- risk-taker
- manager

The successful individual must simultaneously perform well in each role; it is no use, for example, having a marvellous idea and risking all your resources on it only to fail miserably in its practical delivery.

This broad structure is followed in the book but amplified in several significant ways. The conventional analysis offers important insights into such people's business approach and behaviour and, indeed, individual chapters are devoted to each of the above headings. However, that is only part of the story. The missing elements relate to what such people are actually *like* as commercial colleagues, as bosses, as business associates or as husbands, wives or fathers. Our investigation of the 'naked' entrepreneur has, therefore, two additional, and crucial facets.

not only exploits an idea but invents it in the first place

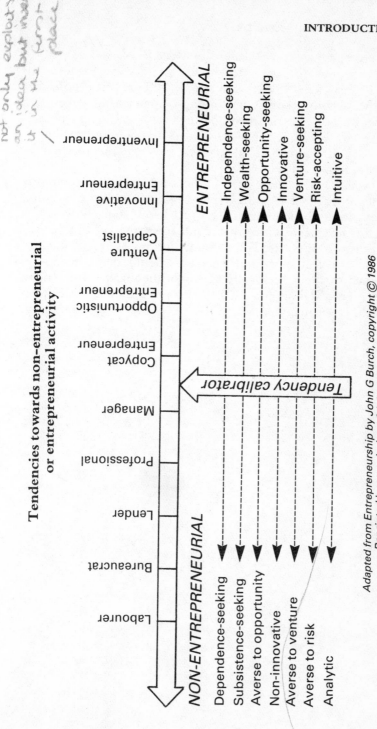

Tendencies towards non-entrepreneurial or entrepreneurial activity

Adapted from Entrepreneurship by John G Burch, copyright © 1986 Reprinted by permission of John Wiley & Sons Inc.

The entrepreneur as *individualist,* and as *prima donna.*

In chapters devoted to these topics, we explore the characteristics that make such people 'different' and how they can be uncomfortable, demanding but inspiring colleagues. Anyone with experience of dealing with entrepreneurs will testify to the importance of understanding the 'chemistry' involved. In these chapters the test tube and microscope are brought into play!

Throughout the text, case studies and examples are used to highlight particular points. They are drawn from personal experience and therefore reflect 'real life'. None, however, is exactly identifiable with any individual or company but they are rather composites based on a number of cases. Any comments, whether critical or complimentary, should therefore not be assumed to apply personally to any of the many entrepreneurs with whom the author has had the privilege and pleasure of working over many years.

Chapter 2

Innovator

Every 'new' business has some element of innovation within it. Opening a new restaurant, starting a garden centre or a pet shop, is innovative as far as the owners are concerned. They are taking business risks and they may well see themselves as being 'entrepreneurs'. It is quite probable, however, that the new venture has little real novelty beyond the location involved and the commendable initiative being taken by the proprietors. True innovation occurs when the venture, product or idea has a striking degree of difference from what has gone before. The change itself might be small: what matters is the extent to which it represents a genuinely new way of doing things.

Take, for example, the case of the McDonald's hamburger chain. Hamburger stores were commonplace in the United States when that company first entered the market-place. They could easily have chosen to adopt a similar formula to their competitors' by offering cheap, no frills, fast food, with success depending on price and location and little else. The management of McDonald's, however, realised that customers would pay a premium price for their hamburger if it was served cheerfully and efficiently, in clean and well-organised outlets to a consistently high quality wherever the consumer saw the McDonald's sign. The innovation involved was therefore not about changing the product but about developing a replicable presentation formula which has now conquered the world. It is this element of insight and novelty which distinguishes the entrepreneurial approach from that of the simple copies.

Peter Drucker in his book *Innovation and Entrepreneurship* has described this process of successful innovation as being 'the specific instrument of entrepreneurship'. In examining the characteristics of the entrepreneur, we must explore both the source of this innovative urge and how it is realised in practice.

Brainwaves and cheap copies

It is easy to confuse innovation with invention. It is often assumed that the innovator is a wild-eyed scientist working at his laboratory bench late into the night to develop some miracle product which will revolutionise our daily lives. Undoubtedly, there are such brilliant individuals who have a genius for finding some previously unthought of solution to a problem, a totally new material or process (bakelite and nylon are examples of the former) or new products which will fundamentally change the way people work or spend their leisure. There is a seemingly endless catalogue of inventive geniuses who have made historic breakthroughs in a whole range of scientific and technological fields: Alexander Graham Bell, Edison, Marie Curie, Cockcroft, Barnes Wallis and Sir Clive Sinclair are just a few of the names which spring to mind. Given their genius for invention it is perhaps surprising to note how few of these illustrious people were ultimately successful as entrepreneurs.

It is equally true that 'invention' in terms of new products and processes is as often as not the result of a team effort involving a number of individuals working over a long period within either an academic institution or a large company – environments not normally associated with entrepreneurialism. The results of their work are, however, often associated with later and highly successful entrepreneurial development, while the individuals in the research team – the true inventors – are seldom direct participants in this second stage.

In the classical sense of being inventors, therefore, it is unwise to assume that entrepreneurs either inevitably need that capability or that those who possess it can complement their inventiveness with the ability to exploit their ideas. Innovation is essentially a creative process but not necessarily one which involves novel products or services. Indeed, it is quite likely that the entrepreneur himself is not a particularly creative person in the conventional meaning of that word.

What are the issues which condition the entrepreneur's ability to innovate and where can we draw the line between the brainwave and the cheap copy?

Looking for the incongruous

Experience suggests that the entrepreneur often has a more vivid and active imagination than his colleagues. He foresees business opportunities in a more realistic and complete form and the consequences of actions which he can take with greater clarity than his peers. Take, for example, the case of the promoter of the hula hoop. There must have been some point at which the person concerned imagined boys and girls on street corners playing with a ring of plastic in a way which was completely novel at the time. His 'vision' must have been sufficiently strong to encourage him to develop and market the product. There are doubtless many similar examples. But what led to that vision in the first place?

The explanation is that entrepreneurs have a restless interest in the incongruous. An incongruity is something which seems to the entrepreneur to be not quite 'right'. It is rather like a flaw that is found by an expert in a fine work of art which is not apparent to the layman. Once he has spotted it, the entrepreneur is not satisfied until he has found a way of making the incongruous 'right' again. For example, he might worry over the proposition, 'Surely there ought to be more for young people to do in this town than going to the cinema' or the problem of 'How do I keep my chrysanthemums from blowing over when it's windy?' His imagination sets to work and his profit motivation is stimulated. Whether they are aware of it or not, entrepreneurs habitually collect information about their environment and review it for such incongruous features. The reason they do this is that incongruous situations offer opportunities for exploitation.

Typically, an incongruity will fall into one of several generic categories:

1. A mismatch between the way something is currently done and how it could be done more effectively using a radically different approach;
2. A poorly satisfied user demand that can be better met by a new product or service;
3. An opportunity for a new venture arising out of some change in the economic, legal or business climate;
4. A recognition of an incipient user demand resulting from the creative application of some new technology.

These four categories can be illustrated from common experience of successful entrepreneurial ventures.

Doing things better

It was not many years ago that the idea of the supermarket was born. Previously, groceries had been sold in small specialist shops on high streets and at street corners. The entrepreneurial opportunity was recognised when the concept of self-service was born. Wage costs formed the dominant part of the overheads of retailers and the breakthrough came from examining ways of employing labour more efficiently and using the savings made to set cheaper prices. Traditionally, the 'assistant' had been the servant of the customer, offering advice, explaining the merits of the product, weighing, slicing or counting it, packing and pricing it. The innovation was to stand this idea on its head. Well-presented, prepacked and priced products do not need sales assistants. The customer 'serves' the shop assistant on the till who must simply total the bill and collect the money. This development led logically to an expansion in store sizes, introduction of the 'own label' concept and the purchasing domination of the major grocery chains. In origin, however, the entrepreneurial idea was simple – 'Let the customer select the product himself and thereby save us labour costs so that we can reduce the price of the article.'

The better mouse-trap

It is often said that the world would beat a path to the door of the man who invented a 'better mouse-trap'. Identifying a conventional process or product and being convinced that it can be carried out or made more efficiently and economically requires, in itself, a leap of the imagination. To follow it through to a successful exploitation requires additional qualities of a quite exceptional order.

Before the introduction of Letraset in 1960, printers and designers used costly and time-consuming methods of hand drawing or cutting out and pasting down type pulls to make up artwork for advertisements, leaflets and the like. 'What if,' speculated Dai Davies, the inventor of the system, 'the old-fashioned child's transfer that you soak in a saucer of water and slide off, could be used for lettering?' At the time, most people regarded such a process as impracticable and Dai had few supporters in his pioneering work. Despite this scepticism, shortages of funds and many setbacks, he showed remarkable dedication to his pursuit of this apparently simple concept. He was convinced that the printing industry was ready for this 'better mouse-trap' and after four years of struggle was able to launch his new product.

The market proved not only receptive to the new idea but

willing to pay a price sufficient to sustain the growth of the Letra-set company over a number of years. It experienced quite a remarkable success and traditional methods were soon super-seded throughout the western world.

The introduction, and increasingly widespread use, of desktop publishing has overtaken many of the applications for Letraset. However, the story of the development of this product, from invention to commercial exploitation, offers a vivid example of the way in which conventional thinking can be challenged by the determined entrepreneur.

A change in the climate

The digging of the Suez canal (completed in 1869) had a dramatic effect on the world shipping industry. The distance saved by using the canal instead of the Cape of Good Hope route on a voyage between northern France or England and Bombay is 7000 km and the canal offers the shortest route between the eastern seaboard of North America and the ports of the Indian Ocean. It was clear from the earliest inception of the project that the canal would have a fundamental effect on the structure and economics of world trade. It was only those more entrepreneurial ship-owning companies who fully realised this potential and organised both fleets and cargoes to take full advantage of it.

A more up-to-date example will be the consequences of the Channel Tunnel and the opportunities which such a structural change will offer those who can clearly envisage the consequential changes in the patterns of business operations.

Creating new demand

The invention of television is a classic example of a product being created to meet a market need which no one previously realised existed. John Logie Baird saw the potential value of transmitting live pictures into people's homes. He saw it as a gap in the available forms of communication rather than offering it as a reaction to a well-articulated public demand. There are many examples of such 'breakthrough' products. The Sony Walkman, the digital watch, the portable computer and the mini-car were all developed on this basis.

How it is done

The entrepreneur sees opportunities to innovate in terms of their potential to make money for him. The process of spotting the incongruities and the opportunities they create varies enormously from one individual to another. For some it is a systematic and painstaking process, carefully documented. For others it is more inspirational and spasmodic. However, all entrepreneurs appear to share the common characteristic of being extremely sensitive to the world about them and particularly capable of creating an 'internal' vision of how it might change if the entrepreneurial idea was pursued to its full extent. In this process there is clearly a role for inspirational brainwaves. Cheap copies, on the other hand, rarely if ever represent genuinely entrepreneurial opportunities.

The entrepreneur is someone who has the insight to spot a business opportunity which has novelty and is innovative. What happens next? Many people have good business ideas, spot the opportunities, see the exploitation potential but do nothing about it. In the case of the entrepreneur, certain special characteristics start to take over and he typically adopts quite a different approach from the rest of us.

Tunnel vision

The words 'obsessive' or 'fixated' are sometimes used to describe the entrepreneurial drive. It is certainly true that many entrepreneurs become so committed to a particular concept or product that in its pursuit their behaviour becomes unconventional, even outlandish. There is a fine line between the behaviour of the dedicated enthusiast and that of the irrational bigot. Successful entrepreneurs avoid being caught in this trap because they know that their success depends on the support and influence of others who are not impressed by extremism. However, they are usually as dedicated to and protective of their idea as any parent defending a child.

The entrepreneur's commitment to his idea is obviously stimulated, at least in part, by self-interest, whether measured in terms of financial reward or personal recognition. The more intriguing element is the almost missionary zeal with which an apparently trivial innovation is pursued. It seems that this stems typically from the entrepreneur's strong sense of independence and a recurring need to demonstrate it through succeeding by his own efforts. A darker interpretation is that this only reflects the entrepreneur's essential insecurity in the face of the world about him and his need to perform exceptionally to leave some sort of mark on it.

Whatever the deeper motives, it is quite clear that the entrepreneur has an astonishing capacity to be dedicated to the idea or product which he is promoting. This shows itself in the tenacity with which he will endure setbacks and failures in the pursuit of his goal, without any apparent loss of enthusiasm or confidence. He does not see this as in any way irrational, but rather accepts that the process of convincing those around him of his own view is more lengthy and troublesome than it should be. Sometimes his patience runs out and persistence turns to irritation. 'Why can't you see it my way?' he may thunder. The fact of the matter is that what is self-evident to him is rarely so obvious to others, who are more concerned with why something *won't* work than why it *will*. Tunnel vision has its advantages – and its drawbacks too.

The thrill of the chase

Entrepreneurs with the capacity to pursue their ideas with unremitting vigour and enthusiasm also have a novel source of personal motivation: that is, the pure enjoyment which many obtain from the process of convincing others of the rightness of their own view. We shall examine later the question of the entrepreneur's view of risk-taking but, whatever the potential rewards, few ventures can succeed without the active support and collaboration of suppliers, customers, bankers and so on.

The process of persuading someone to buy the product, finance the volume or share the risk can be likened to 'the chase'. The target is stalked, cornered, and bagged. The sight of an entrepreneur returning from a foray into the world of finance, having newly converted a doubting banker to his cause, is quite remarkable. The nearest comparable analogy is that of the missionary having newly converted a heathen to the true faith!

A crucial part of this whole process is, of course, the effective communication of the entrepreneur's idea to the people he needs to convince in order to bring it to fruition. This requires salesmanship.

Super salesman

All the available evidence suggests that entrepreneurs come from a wide variety of psychological types, ranging from intuitive extroverts to thinking introverts. To be successful, however, they must share a capability to persuade. When the product or service is itself innovative, the process of persuasion involves a high degree of effective salesmanship.

Some key elements seem to be common to the process and the approach used by successful entrepreneurs. These are:

- a thoroughly researched prospectus;
- an understanding of 'buying' behaviour;
- an ability to present clearly and succinctly.

A clear prospectus

In working through a new idea the successful entrepreneur develops his prospectus in a great degree of detail. Although it is not often written down in such detail, he examines every angle using what might most conveniently be called a 'role-playing' approach. He imagines how he would behave if he were a customer using the new product, what would be involved if he were making it, supplying the raw materials, working in the factory or providing the finance. He imagines what role he, the entrepreneur, would be playing and how he would promote and develop the idea in the market-place. He looks for flaws and difficulties in the argument and although these may never be publicly aired, agonises over the risks of failure and disappointment.

The result of this process is a very complete picture of the project which he wishes to promote. It may take weeks or months to complete: despite their reputation for instant action, successful entrepreneurs rarely rush into new situations. Any major decision is only taken after completing this very detailed and exhaustive analysis process. When influencing others there is always a need for well-documented project information, but this seldom represents more than the tip of the iceberg of this thinking process.

Understanding buying behaviour

Armed with a detailed knowledge of his project, the entrepreneur next assesses the individual interests of the parties that he wants to persuade. When looking at the project from the standpoint of these other people, the key question is, 'What is in it for me?'

Consider, for example, the case of an entrepreneur whose project is to persuade a large library to allow him to take facsimile copies of all their rare books, store them on optical disk and sell the rights of access to this data to academic institutions and publishers. He needs to raise capital for the venture and persuade both the suppliers of the information, namely the library, and the prospective users, that it will be of benefit to them. He must first imagine himself as the chief librarian, custodian of a public institution, deeply conscious of his stewardship responsibilities for a public asset. In dealing with academics and publishing houses he must understand how they are likely to view such an information source, how important it might be to them, and how much they would be prepared to pay for it. Last but not least, he must consider the position of the financier and whether this venture is likely to be interesting from the point of long-term capital gain. He will need to meet all parties during the process of putting his project together and deal appropriately with their concerns and interests. The techniques used in each case would be different: some would be interested in the technology and the status they might gain by being associated with such a venture; others might see an immediate cost advantage or a way of taking an initiative ahead of their competitors. In any event, the entrepreneur must understand the likely buying behaviour of each of his essential collaborators.

In this example, the collaborators are as much buying an idea as a physical product whose characteristics can be easily demonstrated. Selling ideas requires quite different techniques and the really persuasive entrepreneur is able to convey not only a very tangible picture of how his operation would work but also a strongly convincing message about the benefits which would flow to the particular party he is addressing.

This chameleon-like capability to change the whole style and nature of the approach is one of the characteristics enjoyed by many successful entrepreneurs. It extends to the way they use language, gesture and analogy, and remind the listener of previous experience. Taken together, the ability to make a direct appeal in a clear and unequivocal way to the subconscious interest of the 'buyer' is a vital skill possessed by many who are successful in promoting new ventures.

The power to communicate
The communication techniques used by entrepreneurs are many and varied. They are, however, usually more powerful oral than written communicators and the language they employ is often very simple and direct. They tend to make extensive use of

analogy and have the skill to present a complex idea in a straightforward and vivid form. Entrepreneurs seem to draw many of these analogies from childhood and sporting situations. This perhaps reveals a deeper belief that business or enterprise is, itself, a form of sporting activity. They often talk rapidly, using very short and powerful sentences to illustrate an idea. Since optimism is a general characteristic of entrepreneurs, their methods of communication tend to underline this feature.

For example, they often prefer to walk and talk rather than sit quietly behind a desk. Their concentration on the issue in hand is so intense that major distractions, such as loudly ringing telephones or the hubbub of a factory floor, go wholly unnoticed.

When presenting ideas and persuading others, entrepreneurs tend to be better talkers than listeners. Their attention span is often relatively short and they have a tendency to interrupt before others have completed a sentence. Some entrepreneurs use colourful language; few are dry and academic. Hearing an entrepreneur in full flow, 'selling' a new venture to a potential collaborator, is a fascinating and enjoyable experience. It is a brave man, however, who attempts to stand in the path of the verbal bulldozer!

Visionary or profiteer?

The entrepreneur has to be innovative, committed, persistent and persuasive. But what's in it for him? Crude analysis would suggest that there is one simple, overriding and all-persuasive motive – the pursuit of money. But this analysis is inevitably simplistic and the available academic research demonstrates that, although the pursuit of wealth is a powerful influence in the early stages of an entrepreneur's career, its power rapidly diminishes above a certain threshold of achievement. Despite this, the entrepreneur is driven on to greater and greater effort in terms of the energy and commitment which he brings to his role. This 'demon', which appears to stimulate an exceptional response well beyond the stage at which most would be wholly satisfied with their life's work, is worthy of closer analysis.

The following simple and general categorisation of entrepreneurs seems to fit common experience:

- visionaries;
- strivers;
- dealers.

Visionaries

The visionary entrepreneur is spurred on by a general dissatisfaction with the way things are in the world. This is not to suggest that he is a social improver but rather he has a restless conviction that the untidy ends of the world around him can and should be tied up. In search of a better product or service many concerned with technological innovation have a deep-seated conviction that the way things are done now is less than satisfactory. They search for better materials, improved processes, more effective products for the consumer or the industrialist. They appear to have a fairly deep conviction that the world should be an ordered and efficient place and their products and ideas are based on this assumption. In many entrepreneurial initiatives in the service sector the new idea eliminates some previously inefficient part of the system. To be a visionary does not, of course, exclude a genuine desire for profit and capital. Its power as a motivating force, however, persists well beyond the first million pounds, and it appears that those endowed with this quality never lose it. The visionary is the most likely of all entrepreneurial types to be a genuine innovator.

Strivers

Although entrepreneurs are commonly expected to be confident and extroverted, the truth is that many feel both deeply insecure in their relationship with society and a continuing need to prove their capacity to be successful. This is less a case of inadequacy of character than a deep distrust of the permanence of their own achievements. It is curious that the more wealthy and successful some entrepreneurs appear to be, the more paranoid they become about the risk of failure. Even those who achieve secure fortunes far in excess of what they would ever need for total comfort in old age are driven to pile yet more on to their list of achievements and capital.

Such people never seem to be satisfied with what they have achieved. They push themselves relentlessly forward and must always have at least one, and preferably several, new initiatives underway at any one time. They are constantly 'striving' for something which becomes increasingly difficult to determine. They are fiercely competitive and consequently often make poor company when relaxed enjoyment should take precedence over 'winning'. They are exhausting companions, never off duty and always probing and testing new ideas and theories. Generally, they do not seem very happy people: they lack the capacity to relax sufficiently deeply or long enough to benefit from the more enduring human pleasures. The type of venture in which the striving entrepreneur engages is less important to him than the fact of being involved in enterprising ventures. In the extreme anything will do, and such individuals often prefer pure gambling to inactivity.

Strivers, like visionaries, have a restless view of the world. Their interests are likely to be more eclectic in their pursuit of new projects, more obviously driven by their own self-interest. It is from this group of entrepreneurs that the caricature of the distrusting, miserly and egocentric multi-millionaire is drawn.

Dealers

This group is the most dispassionate and calculating of the three. The dealer will look for an opportunity in any market-place, in any country, or in any commodity. He sees his skills as those of being able to act more cleverly, more quickly or more powerfully than his competitors. Typical of this category are entrepreneurs who spot a shortage in one market and an available supply in another, who see unrealised potential in property or who can bring together two parties with a mutual interest. As well as being highly streetwise, they also can be extremely inventive and are often very able judges of people. The financial motive tends to be extremely strong with dealers but once mastered it is often the pleasure of the dealing process which rewards the entrepreneur rather than the financial gain alone. Many very prominent international entrepreneurs show these characteristics very clearly: their company portfolio-building and their aggressive takeover tactics are indicators of this basic approach.

It is worth noting that these categories do not include either gamblers or what might otherwise appear to be normal, level-headed and sensible people. The reason for the exclusion of gamblers is that successful entrepreneurs are seldom if ever serious gamblers. We shall examine this question in more depth in the next chapter.

It is perhaps more difficult to answer the question why the categories do not include normal and level-headed individuals. It would be foolish to deny that many who have developed ideas, exploited them and made fortunes either alone or with teams of colleagues appear to be anything other than normal and level-headed. It can be argued, however, that these apparently calm exteriors conceal powerful internal motivational forces which single out those who genuinely succeed and those who fail. Achievement must, of course, be measured against ambition. The will to make an adequate living through an enterprising venture is wholly commendable. The entrepreneur goes well beyond this modest initial goal and the driving force is powerful and long term.

Summary

Above all, the entrepreneur achieves success through innovation. He looks for the incongruous in the world, treats it as an opportunity and then subjects his vision to detailed and thorough scrutiny. His commitment is coupled with an ability to see the project from the point of view of others and to identify their self-interest during the selling process. Powerful methods of communication are commonplace among successful entrepreneurs who have many of the skills of the effective salesman. They are driven by a wide variety of influences, not least that of the creation of personal wealth. Those who succeed in the long term, however, are subject to complex and interesting motivating forces.

Chapter 3

Risk-taker

All entrepreneurs love to compete. The essence of any competition is that the outcome is uncertain. Hence there is an element of risk and it is the characteristic of the entrepreneur as a risk-taker which we examine in this chapter.

The competitive urge

The bulk of academic research to date confirms the observation that entrepreneurs are abnormally (and sometimes excessively) competitive people. This is often as much apparent in their private lives as in their business activities. For example, anyone who has played golf or tennis against a successful entrepreneur will testify to the aggression which such people bring to their game. Even minor domestic issues are often tinged with the feeling that the entrepreneur not only needs to 'score points' but always wants to have the last word (the personal pronoun 'I' is seldom underused!). There are even situations in which the entrepreneur appears to be competing with himself.

Some already very successful businessmen set themselves what appear to outsiders to be unnecessarily punishing targets. This behaviour can reach extraordinary if not bizarre lengths. In one case, an entrepreneur made promises to his bankers about the outcome of a merger which seemed so extravagant that the deal almost floundered on the spot. He set himself a most daunting task and it required all his energy and ingenuity to complete it. The fact that he did so meant he ultimately won approval and applause from all involved. The more perplexing question is, why did he do it in the first place?

In a famous article in the *Harvard Business Review* ('The Dark Side of Entrepreneurship', November–December 1985) Manfred Kets de Vries argues that the entrepreneur is constantly in search of a way of controlling his environment. Some entrepreneurs, says de Vries, 'are strikingly ambivalent when an issue of control surfaces – they are filled with fantasies of grandiosity, influence, power and authority, yet also feel helpless. They seem to fear that their grandiose desires will get out of control and place them ultimately at the mercy of others.' Winning any competition, however insignificant it may appear, puts the entrepreneur in control of the situation. The scale of the competition, the risks involved and the nature of the prize are less relevant than the driving urge to compete. Taking de Vries's analysis a stage further, entrepreneurs can be seen as deeply insecure individuals with a recurring need to prove themselves to the world around them.

An alternative explanation is more straightforward – namely that entrepreneurs feel naturally superior as individuals and seek every opportunity to prove it. Doubtless, entrepreneurs have a great degree of self-belief and commitment and these qualities are an essential part of their make-up. However, a feeling of natural superiority does not in itself account for the extraordinary lengths to which many successful men and women will go to win at all costs. The much publicised confrontations between highly successful international businessmen seem to be out of keeping with the image of the relaxed, confident and self-assured entrepreneur. It is no coincidence that these people also choose to compete in such fields of sport (the more expensive the better!) as yachting, power boat racing and horse racing. An element of irrationality and personal vendetta sometimes surfaces, doubtless to the concern and discomfiture of the work colleagues: it seems that 'scores' have to be settled almost irrespective of cost and potential benefit.

Undoubtedly, it is the almost obsessive concern for competition which drives the successful entrepreneur towards greater and greater personal achievement. Many companies, both large and small, behave equally competitively in their corporate style. However, this rarely extends to the personal lives of the people involved. Corporate attitudes can change with time and aggressive companies may become complacent as they achieve success. Entrepreneurs by comparison never seem to lose their appetite for new competitive challenges nor their willingness to compete at the personal as well as the corporate level.

The balance of the argument appears to favour the view that entrepreneurs have an abnormally developed need for their achievements to be both within their control and recognised by the world at large. This 'desire for applause' often results in a deep sense of dissatisfaction when the goal itself is obtained. The reason is simple: the value placed on winning by the entrepreneur is very often not accepted by either the people with whom he competes or the team who work with him. They fail to share with him the obsessional desire to succeed and hence the euphoria of winning. Consequently, success itself has a different value and the successful entrepreneur can find that he has a hollow victory on his hands. He usually finds this extremely irritating.

The sporting analogy is helpful once again. If you have competed with someone who is taking the game more seriously than the friendly context requires, you are likely to admire his success but dislike the individual for his attitude to the competition. This can be equally true in business and it is a difficult challenge for the entrepreneur to be both a 'winner' and achieve the genuine applause which he will expect from those around him. It can be done, however, if the 'winner' is mature and self-confident enough to see success in the context of a wider business perspective. It is sometimes a mark of an entrepreneur's 'coming of age' that he tempers his natural inclination to trumpet his achievements at every possible opportunity.

Failure? Who cares!

There is an interesting, almost fundamental, difference in attitude towards business failure in Europe and in the United States. In European countries, business failure is regarded as a major setback in an individual's career. It is seen as not just an unfortunate consequence of the risk-taking process but as prima facie evidence of a fundamental weakness in the person's character. By comparison, the attitude to failure in the United States is quite different. Entrepreneurs are expected (if not required!) to have suffered setbacks and failures as a part of the process of their development as individuals. Business failure is regarded as an essential part of the educational process of an individual ultimately destined to be successful. Risk-taking, whether at personal or corporate level, is seen to be a desirable and necessary part of wealth creation. The higher the risk, the greater the return expected. While this is equally true of his European counterpart, the American entrepreneur appears to have more understanding support from his backers, through both good times and bad. Higher rewards are expected from success (bankers are much larger and more willing company shareholders) but failures are not a cause of major anguish – they are simply seen as a necessary feature of the system.

The apparently more conservative approach to failure in the United Kingdom and elsewhere in Europe suggests greater problems for the entrepreneur in getting his new enterprise off the ground. Although this is now less the case than it was some years ago it is undoubtedly true that here a smaller proportion of ultimately successful businessmen emerge from backgrounds of individual failure than is the case in the United States.

This issue is much influenced by the differing cultures and institutions of the two continents. Many entrepreneurs in the United States emerge from a 'blue-collar' background. By contrast, a study of the British entrepreneur conducted in 1988 (by Cranfield School of Management and Arthur Young) indicated that most of the entrepreneurs in their sample came from families in which the father had some type of small firm or self-employed experience. The educational and social influences therefore have a bearing on the differing attitudes towards failure.

Despite these differences, research suggests that entrepreneurs worldwide share an ability to shake off failure and to start again with a new venture. In the process, many entrepreneurs have the capability to attribute the failure to others rather than themselves. This 'buck passing' seems to be part of a process of insulating the individual from the inevitable self-criticism which would otherwise follow the collapse of the enterprise. Typically, the entrepreneur will blame third parties such as suppliers, bankers, professional managers or accountants who form part of his team. The accusations of misjudgement, incompetence or downright disloyalty are usually expressed in vivid and unequivocal terms. In this way, the entrepreneur preserves his self-esteem (without any particular friends in the process) along with his ability to fight another day.

It is probably an over-simplification to suggest that entrepreneurs do not fear failure with as much passion as they wish for success. The fear itself can be a powerful motivator but there is seldom evidence of it other than through a further adrenalin charge to their generally optimistic approach to the world. Those close to successful entrepreneurs know how much they agonise in private over things which have gone wrong. This is rarely seen in public and never by those on whom the entrepreneur depends for support or patronage.

Although the entrepreneur's attitude to failure may at first appear to be cavalier it can also be regarded as a subconscious reaction to an essential learning process. A child learns about the world by experimenting with it. If one attempt to do something produces failure or pain, another approach is tried, and so on until an effective solution is found. The entrepreneur's impatience to achieve things quickly makes him perhaps more 'accident prone' than his more cautious colleagues.

Although the effect may be educational, the intention of the entrepreneur is unquestionably quite otherwise. It is also arguable whether or not he accepts and recognises what others would conventionally call failure as just that. The very nature of the unconventional way in which entrepreneurs behave makes the commonplace epithets of success and failure generally less applicable to them. In this sense, the entrepreneur sets himself apart from his more conservative colleagues purely because in some mysterious way he seems able to bend, if not break, the rules of conventional life.

Breaking the rules

To be competitive, the entrepreneur frequently feels that he has to manipulate the environment around him to improve the odds on his success. He wants to mark the cards to give him a more favourable chance of winning the game. Indeed, there is a fine line between what is legal (but normally reprehensible) and what is downright dishonest. The well-known saying that 'every great fortune is founded on a lie' contains more than a grain of truth when applied to the fruits of the work of entrepreneurs.

The instinct to shorten the odds by breaking the rules is often no more than a manifestation of a deep suspicion of, or an antipathy towards, anything institutional. It is this very refusal to be bound by the rules which often gives the entrepreneur his competitive edge. What appears to be the genius of highly successful individuals is in fact sometimes no more than a willingness to think from first principles about the nature of a particular problem in order to find a highly unconventional solution.

A famous historical example is the genius that led the Rothschilds to steal a march over their banking contemporaries at the time of the battle of Waterloo. Conventionally, news of victory or defeat in battle was carried by a courier from the battlefield – a process often taking several days, given the state of the roads and sea travel at that time. The Rothschilds realised that there was an alternative means of communication, namely the carrier pigeon. By this means the news of the victory was conveyed in secret to London a day before the conventional reports were received. Gilt-edged stock bought cheaply on rumours of a defeat was sold at massive profits days later when the victory was generally known. Ingenuity or simply a willingness to reconsider the ground rules? Whatever the cause, the effect transformed communications thereafter.

A willingness to break the rules in information-gathering is a common feature of entrepreneurial behaviour. How do entrepreneurs learn about competitive behaviour, for example? They, or their staff, get to know the competitors' employees: they frequent the same pubs, sporting clubs or societies; they approach executives through headhunters and in the process of offering a job to the prospective candidate learn about their competitors' business. They obtain information about their competitors' activities from their own customers and ask them to pass on any information, such as house journals, price lists and product information which they may receive. Stopping short of industrial espionage, the entrepreneur is prepared to use unconventional and unexpected ways of gathering data to obtain a competitive advantage.

The founder of the McKinsey Strategic Management Consultancy came up with a novel way to win a major new client when, in its early stages of development, it was crucial for the business to win a significant account. He rented an apartment next door to that of the owner of his target client and made sure that they met morning and evening as his neighbour left for, and returned from, his office.

This informal contact quickly led to a meeting over dinner at which McKinsey was able to make his business proposal. His competitors, bidding for business through the conventional methods, were outmanoeuvred. This ingenious piece of advantage gaining also quickly changed the methods of consultancy selling in that sector of the market.

When launching new products or services, the entrepreneur will exploit every opportunity to sell benefits which differentiate the venture from competitors – but not always successfully. In the 1970s Freddy Laker pioneered the concept of cheap international air travel, offering the prospect of foreign holidays to an enormous new and untapped market. His entry into that activity promised to create competitive disruption and it appeared for some time that the new enterprise would take the aviation business by storm. Despite the ultimate failure of the venture, the role of Freddy Laker as 'people's champion' is now part of the mythology of the aviation industry. Later operators such as Richard Branson have in many senses been the inheritors of this earlier innovative and rule-breaking initiative.

In launching the ill-fated C5 city car, Sir Clive Sinclair took an equally bold step in offering a revolutionary form of urban transport. His reputation as an inventor and his capability to persuade his backers disguised the reality of the product's shortcomings. There is no doubt that Sinclair found an important angle in relation to pent-up consumer demand; the problem was less in the concept than in the delivery.

Concert parties

Even if a new idea has the most startling and obvious commercial potential to the entrepreneur, he often has to persuade others with more conservative views that the project is viable. The technique commonly used is that of creating an unstoppable momentum for a project by forming what is often called a concert party. In its crudest form, this is simply a manipulation of people's natural desire not to be left out when there is a good thing going. In its more sophisticated manifestation, the entrepreneur understands and manipulates these motives in a very subtle way. A hypothetical situation will illustrate how this is done.

A promoter, Joe Smith, sees the opportunity for an on-line translation service for medium-sized companies. He realises that such companies increasingly do business in foreign countries but have few in-house language skills. Tender documents, correspondence and product literature is commonly referred to local teachers or trade associations for translation, involving time delays and sometimes inadequate understanding of the technical terms used. He envisages a central bureau staffed by experienced linguists using advanced computer techniques to record and recall dictionaries of terms in many languages. The bureau would be linked to individual companies through fax or computer networks so that the customer would be charged both an annual subscription and a transaction fee, depending on the extent to which they used the bureau.

The concept is simple and potentially highly profitable. However, it needs a considerable amount of capital, the support of a 'core' of company users and the availability of sufficient numbers of translators of the required quality. There are therefore three quite distinct groups of people whom the entrepreneur must persuade before the project can start, namely financiers, customers and translators.

Joe starts by talking to companies. He paints a glowing picture of the scale and efficiency of the service, mentions the names of several of their competitors who are interested and promises both cost saving and competitive advantage. He also seeks permission to use their names as potentially interested customers. The companies concerned see little to lose in showing support in principle since they have no contractual obligation. In addition, they are also anxious not to lose out to competitors when promised some degree of exclusivity. Their names are, of course, used by Joe when visiting his next potential customer in such a way that they sound like very enthusiastic supporters of the venture.

Joe then tracks down his potential translators. He tells them that he has the venture almost set up and that he can promise them an interesting and rewarding career. He fills them with enthusiasm at the prospect of senior management appointments and early promotion and gives them a foretaste of share option schemes and capital profit. Carried away by Joe's infectious enthusiasm they cannot wait to sign up.

Armed with these credentials, Joe talks to his potential financiers. He plays the field by involving more than one investor. He hints to each that one of the others is more advanced in the negotiations and can offer better terms. He quotes the venture as a *fait accompli* and his staff as though they were already hired. He has found the premises, the lease must be signed in three days, a major customer has an urgent contract to fulfil . . . Many other similar devices are used to hustle the deal. Joe only needs to put one of the pieces in place to increase the likelihood of assembling the others. He creates an atmosphere of excitement and momentum and, with any luck, the concert party is soon gathered.

As Joe will find, the most difficult person he has to persuade to join in this communal wish fulfilment is the financier, streetwise and case-hardened, who approaches every deal with studied care and caution. Even these prudent individuals, however, have been known to get carried away on the entrepreneurial bandwagon. The high failure rate of new ventures which is widely accepted by the financing community must in part be accounted for by this factor.

Conduct unbecoming

By breaking establishment rules, sailing close to the wind and being generally unpredictable, many entrepreneurs get a reputation for being less than respectable. Any market which has become institutionalised and comfortable is fair game for the raiding entrepreneur. In such a situation competitors commonly observe a strong unwritten ethical code. This is not to suggest that cartels exist, but rather that a state of gentlemanly equilibrium is observed between competing parties. Whoever is bold enough to challenge this ordered situation will inevitably be branded as, at best, a disreputable maverick. This description is almost always unfair and no more than a cry of pain from those whose cosy world is challenged, perhaps for the first time.

It was an entrepreneurial initiative which shook the established world of the high street grocery stores with the coming of the supermarket; ship owners were wrong-footed by the introduction of the container ship and the supertanker; the ingenuity and aggression of Japanese electronics' manufacturers shocked many European companies into a sudden awareness of their own innate weakness.

Acting as a catalyst for radical change in such mature and well-established situations, the entrepreneur is bound to find himself regarded as ungentlemanly and his activities unwelcome. The interesting question is whether entrepreneurs intentionally seek such confrontation with the established order or whether it is an incidental feature of their drive to succeed.

Research into the attitudes of entrepreneurs in the United States and Europe suggests that they feel deeply uneasy in a well-ordered setting. Many entrepreneurs drop out of school early or find themselves at odds with the boss in a working context. They have the reputation of being 'against the system', questioning decisions and making life difficult for their superiors. They demonstrate their independence through many, apparently trivial, aspects of their behaviour: at school they may be poor attenders, insolent to teachers or leaders of playground gangs; at work they may have the tiresome habits of questioning decisions, poking their noses into aspects of the business which do not immediately concern them and making trouble on the shop floor; in their leisure time they may seek activities which involve potential conflict with authority. While this non-conformist approach to life varies in degree of prominence between entrepreneurs, as a general rule it appears to be one of their distinguishing characteristics. Certainly, those who have been successful in the long term often show this predilection to challenge the established order to a high degree.

A feeling of unimportance?

Some psychologists have argued that entrepreneurs need to reassure themselves constantly of their importance in the world. In a sense, this is a manifestation of a deeply-felt inferiority complex. By taking on challenging and risky situations the entrepreneur draws attention to himself and thereby enhances his self-esteem. Although this analysis has some merit (and experience suggests that entrepreneurs are not always the bold, confident individuals that they project themselves to be) there seems an equal likelihood that the motive is as much mischievous as attention-seeking. The pure pleasure which an entrepreneur can gain from the discomfiture of those whom he regards as established and self-satisfied has to be seen to be believed. It is this iconoclasm which often makes entrepreneurs exciting and agreeable to work with.

The 'magnificent obsession' which spurs entrepreneurs on to break the rules can also lead them into darker areas of deceit and wrong-doing. There is a line which entrepreneurs sometimes find very difficult to discern between 'conduct unbecoming to a gentleman' and conduct that can lead to the prison cell. It is very easy, when challenging the established order, to create a personal set of rules which stray over this narrow line. Trading practices which may be unconventional but acceptable are quite different from those which break the law. This is not to suggest that entrepreneurs are less ethical or honest than anyone else. It is simply that they place themselves in situations where the temptation to act dishonestly is greater than usual.

For example, an entrepreneurial property developer seeking planning consent for a speculative investment in land which has stretched his financial resources may well be tempted to go beyond simple persuasion when dealing with council officials. His entrepreneurial drive has put him into the situation where the issue of one person's attitude to the transaction may be crucial to his future. This self-imposed pressure does, sometimes, lead the entrepreneur towards the slippery slope of illegal behaviour. Part of his difficulty may be the lack either of an external set of values to which he adheres sufficiently strongly or the confidence in an adviser who has such values. This in itself can be a product of the entrepreneur's tendency to be a non-conformist. Thus he may find himself in a position where his judgement of what is right or wrong in a situation is conditioned more by his own view of the world than by any dispassionate analysis of legality. The 'crimes' committed by entrepreneurs are probably more associated with misrepresentation through exaggeration than culpable acts of dishonesty. In this respect, they have only themselves to blame for their often poor public image.

In most things, the entrepreneur is a risk-taker. Finding a competitive edge or a novel approach to a problem involves assessing risks. How does the entrepreneur go about this vital process?

Knowing the odds

Every businessman knows that the assessment of a commercial risk is an art rather than a science. Although economists, mathematicians and accountants can offer powerful techniques to illuminate the decision, the final judgement is inevitably subjective. The reason is simple: the world is highly complex and political, economic and commercial forces interplay both nationally and internationally in ways which remain poorly understood. Any enterprising venture, whether by an individual or a corporation, inevitably involves uncertainty associated with forces well beyond rational analysis. All businessmen must use whatever intellectual skills they have in understanding analytical data to complement their powers of subjective judgement. In sporting terms, the businessman is thereby taking the best view he can of the odds on success against failure. The entrepreneur must address the same issues to reach his own conclusions on the potential for success. His approach, however, often differs radically from that used in large corporations. It generally has the following features:

- extremely sensitive understanding of customer behaviour;
- a strongly visualised understanding of operating parameters;
- a very detailed (and often cautious) assessment of downside risks.

Each of these is worth examining in more detail.

Knowing the customer

The entrepreneur's customers may be companies or individuals and the product or the service offered may be an exploitation of an existing idea or the introduction of a new one. There may be a few, highly specialised, potential buyers or every teenager with money in his pocket – the permutations are endless. The successful entrepreneur has gained an insight into the way that the market is likely to behave *after* his project is launched, not just how it behaves today.

There are three distinctive ways in which this sensitivity to the customer's need is achieved:

1. keen observation of human behaviour;
2. an eclectic interest in information; and
3. a powerful imagination.

The ability to be a keen observer does not necessarily involve high intellect; it is more an inborn sense of curiosity. Spotting a business opportunity, as discussed earlier, requires an acute sense of the 'missing links' or inconsistencies in the way things are presently done. This same sensitive power of observation also feeds the judgemental processes involved in risk-taking. The entrepreneur is almost like a medieval explorer stepping for the first time on to the shores of an unknown continent: he has a heightened awareness of his surroundings because they are both alien and potentially both exciting and dangerous. The entrepreneur, always questioning the existing order, could be seen to have heightened perception for a not dissimilar reason. By contrast, those whose inclination is more towards a comfortable conformity are less likely to be acute observers of human behaviour. They expect people to behave in predictable ways and rarely question the degree to which changed opportunities will themselves result in different behaviour patterns.

It is the behavioural observations which are, of course, crucial. Many entrepreneurial plans are based on what appears to be the wholly rational – 'If I can make this product with more features than my competitors for 10 per cent less, I will sell a hundred thousand a year.' In the long run such rational arguments are often totally valid, so that the replacement of the penny-farthing bicycle by the two-wheeler was an inevitable consequence of the superior efficiency of the latter. The flaw lies in the assumption of rationality in the short term, over which period entrepreneurial success or failure is frequently measured.

Even in the most apparently clinical and quantified areas of business, such as banking, insurance and stockbroking, buying behaviour, when it comes to innovation, is determined by factors other than the purely rational. An individual's judgement on whether to follow an innovative lead will be determined by many things – not least by his innate conservatism or radicalism, the choices of competitors and peer group members, the internal politics of the vested interest in his own organisation and so on. At the individual level, the dictates of fashion and snob appeal are often more powerful influences over consumer choices than anything which would otherwise be a rational determinant. Thus anyone associated with innovation must reckon with these irrational elements in human behaviour. By keenly observing the way people behave in one set of circumstances, the entrepreneur can better predict how they will behave in another. An example will serve to illustrate this point.

Ted Tweedle has invented the ultimate robot, the electronic manservant which will not only do the housework to your oral commands but will serve drinks to your guests, tell bedtime stories to the children and dig the garden. The price is steep but the potential market is huge. Ted's problem is to make some accurate prediction of how quickly his product will take off. A crucial issue is how the robot is sold; it can be retailed through high street chain stores, sold in the customer's own home, or marketed by mail order. Each selling situation suggests a different behavioural response, so Ted uses his observation of analogous situations to decide which would be best.

He has observed that the larger domestic items are bought from retail stores by husband and wife together. The wife, as primary user, normally leads the choice with the husband as the final arbiter and paymaster. In the home setting, by contrast, the husband is usually the dominant individual in the buying process, perhaps because there is a subconscious assumption that he will act more dominantly in his own domain. Lastly, he knows that selling large items by mail order lacks any 'feel' beyond what the customer (husband or wife) sees on the printed page.

His experience tells him that the buying decision is more likely to be made by the husband than the wife. Quite apart from the cost of the robot he observes that, if a radical change is involved, the person with most potential to benefit is often the most reluctant to initiate the change. He therefore seeks the setting in which he can maximise the likelihood of the husband making a positive buying decision. He bases his assumptions, therefore, on the sale of the robot to potential customers in their own homes.

The information gatherer
The ability to observe behaviour keenly and in detail is often complemented by a broad-ranging and almost magpie-like affection for collecting data. Recent research has shown that successful business leaders ask between 500 and 1000 questions during an average working day. These questions are asked not only of immediate subordinates but of a huge network of people both inside and outside the organisation. The sponge-like quality of absorbing what may seem to be irrelevant data from all sorts of sources, storing it away and being able to retrieve it when needed is a very recognisable trait. Many entrepreneurs read very little and most seem to read less and less the more successful they become. They rely on what they hear or see with their own eyes. Some commit little to writing and appear to distrust anything that cannot be expressed in strong and simple language.

These two qualities of keen observation and eclectic interest in information-gathering is often coupled with a powerful imagination. Entrepreneurs do not need to be imaginative in the wholly creative sense of that word. Much of entrepreneurialism is concerned with exploiting opportunities and ideas which are derived from those of others. However, the power of imagination applies to a more logical process which flows directly from these two other talents. Thus, for example, the promoter of a new chain of ethnic restaurants might visualise not only the sort of customers to whom the food would appeal but the physical location, the interior door, the style of service, the promotional programme and so on. Very often, it is that imaginative power which gives the entrepreneur the ability to exploit ideas which have lain fallow after the initial phase of invention. It is almost as though the creative process becomes spent and a new innovative charge is needed. For many years the inventiveness of British technology has been exploited in other countries. The hovercraft is probably the best-known example of both the difference and the synergy between creativity and entrepreneurial exploitation. The imagination of the entrepreneur must not stop short at the product itself – it has to visualise the ultimate use and its associated revenue flow.

Seeing all the parts

There is risk attached to every aspect of a new venture. The old adage has it that 'the battle was lost for the want of a horse-shoe nail'. Similarly, a business venture can be wrecked by the failure of an apparently insignificant but vital element. Any complex new product is likely to involve a variety of technologies and sources of supply. Poor quality, late delivery or unexpectedly high costs of any can be disastrous. Unsuccessful ventures in recent years in three-dimensional photography and 'fourth generation' television are striking examples.

The successful entrepreneur must not only understand the individual elements of his project but he must have the ability to see them as the interlinked parts of a complete enterprise. A vital element is the collaborators, managers and employees who will bring the idea to fruition. The entrepreneur must perceive both their individual roles and also the way in which they are likely to relate to each other. He must face the risks of poor recruitment as much as the possibility of a supplier or subcontractor letting him down.

The process involved in refining this operating model goes on largely inside the entrepreneur's head. It appears to be an iterative series of postulations based on adjusting one factor at a time and considering the consequences of that on the project as a whole. For example, he may consider the effects of making a product in-house or simply assembling bought-in components. What effect will this have on factory management, stock levels, customer deliveries, finance requirements, profit margins and so on? Next, he will consider part manufacture and part bought-in components and go through the same sequence of considerations. Some variations will have several dimensions of influence on the venture. Choosing to sell direct or through wholesalers is one illustration of how a venture will differ fundamentally in its operation. It is a complex process which has been likened to solving the problems of four-dimensional chess. What may appear to an outsider to be a near-miraculous feat of organisation when a project is started is often merely a manifestation of this highly detailed and time-consuming thought process which has been going on in the entrepreneur's mind for some time. We will look in a later chapter at the role of the entrepreneur as a planner and manager; in many ways this ability to 'exploit' a concept, which the original inventor perhaps found too difficult, is one of his key differentiating skills.

It is rare to find this process either fully documented or employing conventional risk measurement methods. Once again, the entrepreneur's judgement of how people in a new context are likely to react is an essential element. As most management scientists would agree, the uncertainty involved is considerable. The entrepreneur relies on the information-gathering and assessment of needs which we discussed earlier as a vital ingredient in this process. It must also be both comprehensive and thorough down to the finest detail. For example, launching a new product might involve the following key elements:

- securing the supply in adequate quantities and to reliable quality of all key components;
- finding a suitable manufacturing location and facilities;
- recruiting suitably expert management and training a labour force;
- obtaining the necessary funds both to start the venture and to finance it through its initial launch period;
- devising marketing and selling plans and preparing launch programmes;
- conducting relevant market research to confirm the entrepreneur's assessment of the likely uptake of a new product; and

- maintaining the maximum secrecy practicable before the launch itself.

Although the motor industry is dominated by large manufacturers, the preparation and launch of a new model involves many of these elements. Using this analogy, it is clear that failure to anticipate and deal with difficulties in any of these areas could be both costly and potentially crucial to the success of the enterprise.

Every project is, of course, different in its complexity and there are many illustrations of entrepreneurial ventures which are no more than 'acorns', where the principle of a modest test launch is the most viable approach. Even there, however, the entrepreneur who has not thought through all the aspects of the venture is running additional risks, not only on his own behalf but also for those who are backing him. It is the person with the capacity to see all the parts of a venture and to review how each interacts with the other who is most likely to succeed. The techniques used are sometimes referred to as 'scenario planning' and many corporate strategies are now based on the more formal use of this technique. It is an interesting illustration of how the entrepreneurial model infects the management disciplines used by those involved in more mature businesses.

Assessing the downside
Entrepreneurs are commonly assumed to be risk-takers to the extent that they are willing to gamble on any situation. It is sometimes cynically suggested that they are more than happy to play with other people's money, with the object of achieving both self-esteem and exceptional gain. Gambling can involve either a blind faith in good fortune or a close assessment of risks. Experience suggests that most entrepreneurs are remarkably cautious in their approach to risk-taking, despite the fact that the initiatives they take are seen by others as bold and adventurous.

The reason for this paradox is that the conscious or subconscious analysis which the entrepreneur makes when he is looking forward to a new project involves a process of confidence-building based on his own judgement. There is a regular reassessment of the downside risk involved in the project; thus the exposure (usually measured in financial terms) involved should any part of the project fail is quantified and, if appropriate, accumulated with those relating to other elements.

In the case illustrated on page 47, the risk analysis is being undertaken for a contractor who is aware that there are various major factors affecting finishing the job on time (each of these is listed at the foot of the chart). The vertical axis measures the probability of an event occurring by a particular date – when it is 0 the event cannot occur before then and when it reaches 1 it is certain to occur.

Each of the six factors is considered in turn, the measurement of the probability of each being *added* to produce a combined maximum delay for the project as a whole until the end of September. The intersection between the base plan completion date line and line 6 (representing the accumulated risk) intersects at 0.2 indicating that there is only a 20 per cent chance that the contractor will be able to complete his project on time. He must then decide whether to accept the degree of risk involved, negotiate a new, later, completion date or renegotiate the penalties for late completion of the contract.

The diagram illustrates in graphical form how the risk inherent in a project can be measured and the cumulative effect judged.

Risk-management techniques are commonly used in civil engineering projects, for example in the building of a dam. Before the project starts there are uncertainties about the soil conditions to be encountered, the weather during the construction period, the volume of materials needed to construct the dam to a given height, the possibility of labour unrest and so on. The risk-measurement technique involves a very scientific and careful assessment of previous experience in other projects, the judgement of experts and the expression of the results in terms of statistical confidence levels. By aggregating the risk assessments, an overall risk coefficient can be calculated for the project and converted into a bracket of both time and project cost. If the project is destined to be directly revenue-earning, such as a new toll bridge, the risk-assessment model can be linked directly to the income assumptions. Thus a delay in the completion date of a project both extends the expenditure period and reduces the net present value of the income because it is received later than originally planned. These differences alter, in turn, the expected rate of return on the project and may indeed reach a point at which its viability comes into question.

Whatever method is used, the promoter of a project must see a *comparative* risk–reward ratio which is acceptable to him. In the case of a project being considered by a mature company, there are two criteria by which this measurement is made:

1. the external opportunities to invest at a comparable level of risk; and
2. competing internal projects.

If a company is considering whether or not to invest in the development and launch of a new product with an 80 per cent chance of success then it must show at least a 20 per cent better return on capital than, say, a totally safe investment in government bonds. Equally, if there is competition in the company between two possible ventures, the one offering the more attractive risk–reward equation will normally be chosen. In this way, commercial judgements in established companies are, in theory at least, justified in terms of both offering a better return than an alternative external investment and the best internal candidate available. In practice, there are often much broader and more subjective issues of corporate strategy involved in investment decisions than this rather mechanical approach would suggest. It nonetheless remains an essentially comparative process and it is this which provides the insight into the way in which the entrepreneur approaches risk.

Richard Branson, when describing his own approach to risk, says that he keeps each of his enterprises small and never takes a business risk which would put any of his other ventures in jeopardy. This limiting of the downside is, in his case, the feature of a well-organised and mature entrepreneurial business. When a new business is started the downside is often the financial ruin of the entrepreneur – indeed, those supporting a new venture expect the promoter to back it with all his available capital, time and energy. It would seem logical that an entrepreneur, faced with this apparently huge risk, would only choose those ventures which offered an exceptional payback. Optimistic self-delusion, however, can infect the judgement of the entrepreneur to the extent that he dismisses risk and sees nothing but immeasurable reward. Perhaps in some cases it is irrational self-confidence which turns the venture that flies in the face of common sense into a historic success story. However, for every case in which this happens there are a thousand where it doesn't.

The first venture which an entrepreneur undertakes is almost certainly motivated more by the very strong ambition of the individual to become independent and recognised by those around him as a success than by any more rational considerations. Measured by external alternatives, these first entrepreneurial ventures appear to be poor investments. Indeed, many fail and

Cumulative risk profile

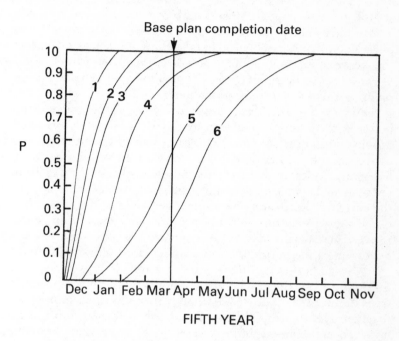

Cumulative probability distribution with six risk source components for a construction project. The components are:
1. Yard not available/mobilisation problems
2. Construction problems/adverse weather
3. Late delivery of subcontracted items
4. Material delivery delays
5. Industrial disputes
6. Delayed award of contract

P = probability coefficient where 1 = certainty

Adapted from Cooper & Chapman, *Risk Analysis for Large Projects* 1986. Reprinted by permission of John Wiley & Sons, Ltd.

47

the venture capitalist is fortunate if, out of his portfolio of ten start-ups, two achieve really significant growth over five years. The 20 per cent who are successful may just have a better proposition, be more capable businessmen, or simply have more good fortune than the others; or it may be that they are just more skilful in assessing the risks and organising their projects accordingly. The entrepreneurs who survive this first venturing phase and prosper rarely need to take comparable levels of risk as the venture matures. Their success attracts opportunities for *leverage,* which becomes the key to making an acceptable return on investment a truly exceptional one.

'Leverage' is the term used to describe the relationship between the equity capital invested in a venture and borrowed money. The equity capital is wholly at risk and is entirely lost if the venture fails. Borrowed money, on the other hand, frequently has some underpinning security to which the lender can have recourse if the venture gets into trouble. In the earlier stages of the entrepreneur's career he is unproven and his ideas, however excellent, will be treated as being more risky than when he has proved his success. As a consequence, his opportunities for borrowing are significantly limited in relation to his own capital.

As he demonstrates his business capability he will attract a following from those who are willing to lend on a substantial basis in return for, perhaps, a small part of the equity. Suppose, for example, that the entrepreneur needs to raise £10m for his new venture; £5m might be covered by some security (say land and buildings), the remaining £5m being largely at risk. If he is established and successful he might do a deal on the basis of, say, £1m of his own money plus £4m of loan capital which could, at the option of the lender, be converted into 10 per cent of the equity of the company. This option will be worth exercising if the value of the company exceeds £40m, since the 10 per cent equity stake will be worth more than the value of the repayment of the loan. At that stage the entrepreneur's original £1m stake would be worth £36m since he still owns 90 per cent of the equity. Up to the point when the option to convert is exercised, the entrepreneur enjoys *all* the equity value even though he has only put up effectively one-fifth of the risk capital.

The more successful the entrepreneur, the greater the opportunity he has to use the leverage effect and the smaller the proportion of equity incentive which he needs to offer his backers. In theory, he can take greater and greater risks since his own proportion of the investment is so small. In practice, however, the house of cards can easily collapse if the entrepreneur does not sustain his reputation as 'a winner'. This brings us back to Richard Branson's approach of restricting downside risks to manageable units. It underlines the reality of the caution which successful entrepreneurs bring in practice to their investment decisions. They are, in effect, hugely aware of the penalty in terms of borrowing capacity which follows in the wake of failure. If their investments are highly leveraged they do not have to seek the level of risk – reward ratio needed by those who lack that reputation. This, perhaps, explains the paradox of the cautious entrepreneur.

Summary

The entrepreneur has an instinctive and powerful urge to compete. He will seek any feasible way to obtain competitive advantage and is a natural rule-breaker. He is prepared to 'sail close to the wind' and use unconventional persuasive techniques. In the last analysis, however, the idea of the entrepreneur as a person who always takes high risks is a myth. The leverage which the entrepreneur can bring to the use of his own capital is the key to his sustaining success while being both thorough and cautious in his assessment of viable projects.

Chapter 4

Individualist

Entrepreneurs thrive on being visible. They like to be 'up front', setting the pace and being recognised. When successful, they welcome the public awareness which follows. Even the least well-read man in the street knows of Robert Maxwell, Tiny Rowland and Richard Branson and can describe some of their attributes. They are individuals with distinctive and very different personalities and styles despite the common success they have achieved in their chosen fields. Do such men set out to be different, and if so what is the mainspring of this drive? Is it, perhaps, that the process of unrelenting competition sharpens and accentuates their individuality? Or are they simply playing out some heroic myth – a source of personal destiny determining the course of the individual's life and career?

The answers to these questions lie deep in the distinctive psychology of the entrepreneur. Although differing in degree and emphasis, the results of academic research and those of ordinary observation confirm that there are many common features. In this chapter these are reviewed and explored.

The rebellious urge

Entrepreneurs generally rebel against rules and authority, whether in school or in the workplace. As Kets de Vries* comments:

> 'While managers seem able to identify in a positive and constructive way with authority figures using them as role models, many of the entrepreneurs I have observed lack the managers' fluidity in changing from a superior to a subordinate

*'The Dark Side of Entrepreneurship' (*Harvard Business Review* November–December 1985)

role; instead they often experience structure as stifling. They find it very difficult to work with others in structured situations unless, of course, *they* created the structure and the work is done on *their* terms.'

This lack of tolerance of, and impatience with, the conventional is a recurrent and marked feature of entrepreneurs. This does not suggest that all rebels are entrepreneurs, but a degree of willingness to 'buck the system' and challenge authority is a recognisable part of the latters' make-up. Stories abound of nascent entrepreneurs who were the terrors of their classrooms, universities or workplaces. Disobedience, disloyalty, a tendency to be at the forefront in any disruptive behaviour are all regularly reported attributes of such youthful mavericks.

There are two schools of thought about why such behaviour occurs. One suggests that the individual has an inborn rebellious urge and the other that it results from 'conditioning'. The first draws on evidence which seems to show that a high proportion of entrepreneurs display this tendency at such an early age that the conventional social factors (class, family background, economic circumstances and so on) have had little, if any, opportunity to be a real influence. They also point out that entrepreneurs spring from a wide variety of backgrounds and few common influences seem to be at work. The 'conditioners' use evidence that entrepreneurs are more often 'incubated' in some environments than others. For example, companies which are themselves entrepreneurial are more likely to spawn individuals with that characteristic than those with a more bureaucratic outlook. Both schools agree that entrepreneurs are confident, self-reliant individuals who have a higher 'locus of control' than people generally. They 'believe that success depends on their own efforts, instead of seeing themselves as victims of luck, chance or fate'.*

Those who support the conditioning theory argue that the circumstances which create the entrepreneurial opportunity must not only be propitious for some new initiative but exactly right as far as the individual is concerned. In effect, the entrepreneur has to be in the right place at the right time in his career for the magic to work. Without this 'accidental' coincidence of opportunity, man and the moment, the prospective entrepreneur never emerges as a real one.

*Longenecker, McKinney & Moore, 'Egoism & Independence: Entrepreneurial Ethics' (*Organisation Dynamics* October 1988). Reprinted, by permission of publisher © 1988. American Management Association, New York. All rights reserved.

It seems that neither school has a complete and convincing answer. The population of entrepreneurs is as wide as is the nature and scale of the enterprises in which they are involved. Within the terms of the definition used in this book, however, successful entrepreneurs seem not only to have an abnormal inclination to be rebellious but also to have shown this trait from an early age. This suggests that there is, perhaps, more of an inherited process at work than one which is externally created.

Whether entrepreneurs are born or made, the fact is that they are often difficult employees and unpredictable workmates. Again, there are three basic explanations which can be broadly described as:

- the applause theory;
- the insecurity theory; and
- the 'other world' syndrome.

Applause-seeking

This theory suggests that the rebellious entrepreneur is motivated by the adulation that challenging the conventional order will win him among his peers. He has a deep fear of being 'ordinary', of not standing out from the crowd and consequently seeks every opportunity to put himself forward. The action may be reckless, spontaneous and even against his own interest but it is, nevertheless, instinctive. Thus, for example, the entrepreneur may set out to shock or outrage his audience if that is the only way of being visible. At a dinner party, the self-made man will want to be heard. If the conversation is out of his field or his fellow guests are standoffish, he will as soon say or do something offensive (insulting the host or committing some other solecism) as not do anything at all. The wife of such a person will testify to the agonies of uncertainty which can precede such events!

Being 'applauded', therefore, does not only mean being congratulated or admired: the applause-seeker gains the same satisfaction from being able to say, 'That showed them' as 'They loved me!' Not all entrepreneurs are as boorish and publicity-seeking as this analysis would suggest, but, there seem to be few successful entrepreneurs who are reluctant to stand out from the crowd. It can be argued, of course, that 'applause-seeking' is no more than another manifestation of the entrepreneur's deeply competitive instinct. It seems that what is instinctive becomes habitual, in terms of social and business behaviour, and it is this feature which results in so many entrepreneurs being disagreeable companions.

The insecurity factor

The second explanation for this rebelliousness is that the entrepreneur is so deeply insecure in his relationship with the world that his actions are aimed at giving him regular reassurance of his importance in it. It is rather like someone walking through a darkened room: hands and feet seek contact, any contact, with the furniture, walls, doors to give a sense of reality to the experience. The insecure individual can, of course, react to this feeling by withdrawing into an increasingly personal inner world but such introversion is very rare in entrepreneurs. The action that gives rise to the desired reassurance is less relevant than the fact that it takes place. Being noticed is more easily achieved through doing something extreme than through doing something essentially ordinary: the eccentric, iconoclastic, rebellious act therefore comes more naturally than the conventional.

It would be foolish to suggest that entrepreneurs are somehow always abnormal or deviant in their psychological make-up, but it seems that many see the world or their personal position in it as somehow incongruous and hence needing correction. The insecurity theory is based on such a premise. The individual rebels less because he feels superior to others but rather because of his discomfort at the *differences* he perceives which others may not. Entrepreneurs seldom come across as insecure people although this characteristic sometimes emerges in later life when fortunes have been made and the competitive pace slackens. It may be that a natural gift for presentation and salesmanship disguises deeper worries than are anywhere publicly apparent.

The 'other world'

There is a theory that certain people see the world in very different terms from the rest of us. They have a comprehensive framework of beliefs, rules, expectations and assumptions which are internally consistent but tangential to those which most people accept and understand. The 'Alice in Wonderland' logic of these other worlds is so self-evident to the individual that things which seem otherwise normal are, to them, extraordinary. Such 'other worldliness' can relate to ethics, value systems, personal relationships, loyalties, political attitudes and numerous other aspects of life.

It is, of course, quite common to find individuals with strongly developed prejudices or personal beliefs. Thus, for example, someone may have a view of personal justice or ethical behaviour which will verge on the extreme. He will stand up against authority when he perceives an injustice being done. He will subscribe to causes, agitate, offer himself for martyrdom or whatever is needed to pursue what he sees as being 'right'. Progress has often depended on the passion and commitment of such people, not least in the fields of religion, politics and the law. Some entrepreneurs share such passions and, as discussed elsewhere, these are frequently the mainspring of their ability to innovate and wreak changes in the world around them.

A passionate set of beliefs about one set of issues does not, however, constitute the whole 'other world'. They are only a part of it. The other world as seen by the entrepreneur must be complete to satisfy this requirement. It would need coherent and consistent views on:

- the order of society and the role of the individual within it;
- what constitutes 'good' and 'bad' behaviour;
- the destiny of the entrepreneur himself and the value of his powers and skills in relation to everyone else; and
- a concept of the 'correct' order of things against which actual experience can be measured.

It can be argued that despotic leaders have many of these delusions and live within a personal and very different set of values from the rest of us. The passionate commitment that they bring to their life's work is testament to the power of this vision. Entrepreneurs are, themselves, quite frequently described as despotic by their subordinates. In some cases the description is used almost as a term of affection and, as much of history demonstrates, a substantial proportion of the human race accepts despotism willingly if not enthusiastically.

What succeeds in politics or religion, however, is unlikely to succeed consistently in business. The 'other world' theory ultimately fails the test of practicality. In the last analysis, the entrepreneur must deliver practical solutions through an understanding and exploitation of human behaviour. Although the politician may also do this, his approach is fundamentally different. The entrepreneur must exploit the opportunities presented by a small part of an existing system. The politician seeks power through manipulating the rules of the system as a whole.

The answer to the question, 'Why does the entrepreneur rebel?' lies not in any one of these theories but, to a greater or lesser extent, in all of them. His behaviour may be irrational and challenging for many reasons, and as a result of complex inner and external pressures. The fact that such behaviour is consistently found cannot be denied. Our ability to analyse its causes, however, remains imperfect.

Whom do I trust?

As fierce competitors, entrepreneurs, particularly early on in their careers, regard everyone as a potential rival. In the school playground, in the factory or office or on the sports field no quarter is sought or expected. A rival is naturally someone who is out to beat you and the last person with whom you share confidences. Experience of the world quickly persuades the entrepreneur that games, whether sporting or commercial, are often not played according to the Queensberry rules. Respect for rivals becomes tinged with and then centred on distrust.

Two individuals may, for example, be bidding for the same piece of work or for the same business opportunity. They may or may not have competed before. Assume that they have broadly comparable solutions to offer at similar prices. The search for individual advantage is therefore likely to turn to other, less conventional considerations. In gaining such advantage, secrecy and surprise are often essential elements. Equally, diversionary tactics may be used. One bidder may leak to the other the fact that he is uninterested in the work or is bidding in the wrong way. Simultaneously, he may have a surprise element in the offing. (A major consultancy assignment in Africa was won, for example, by one bidder promising to transport all the clients' senior executives and their wives to a week's training conference in Florida; their lower priced competitors were totally unaware of this surprise tactic until it was too late!)

In situations such as this the entrepreneur will not only distrust his competitor but also many of his associates and advisers. Playing it close to the chest or 'needing to know' is a commonsense protection against sensitive information falling into the wrong hands. There are many cases, however, where the perceived need for secrecy (and hence the implication of distrust) extends well beyond the boundaries of commercial necessity.

Beyond this narrow and well-defined area of commercial rivalry lies a wider spectrum of personal and commercial relationships in which the grounds for apparently distrusting those around the entrepreneur become more complex and fascinating. The extent of the distrust and hence the degree of loneliness seems to increase dramatically as the entrepreneur himself succeeds and accumulates wealth. The ultimate archetype is the reclusive multi-millionaire, trusting no one, believing himself to be the victim of a predatory conspiracy, miserable and unloved, finally dying unmourned by the rest of the world. Protecting one's hard-won wealth is usually regarded as a natural and creditable action. It is only in the extreme that it becomes somewhat pathetic.

Young, applause-seeking businessmen like to talk about the ventures and the successes they achieve. While they distrust rivals, they are avid information-gatherers and will often take complete strangers into their confidence if there is something to be gained. They seldom leave key tasks to others, although this probably has more to do with lack of confidence in their subordinates' competence than with doubts about their loyalty or motivation. In a sense they have little to lose and so take more conscious (and unconscious) risks.

As an empire grows and wealth is created there is more to protect and the suspicion that people may be trying to cash in on it grows apace. The sense of distrust becomes deeply rooted and can extend as much to close relatives as to business associates. The motives of wives, children, uncles, aunts, nephews and nieces may be questioned in terms of their 'getting their hands on my money'! What applies in the family is often seen in a more extreme way in business.

To counter his mistrust of others, the entrepreneur may divide information about his affairs among a number of people so that no one person can comprehend it all; he may run a management regime on the basis of frequent moves among senior personnel to ensure that no individual becomes too powerful for too long; he may constantly reorganise and restructure his businesses as much to confuse external enquirers as to make his affairs more efficient or tax-effective.

What often emerges is the single 'confidant' who provides the exception to these general rules. There seems to be a curiously wide variety of individuals who play this role. In one real life instance it was a fortune-teller, visited monthly by the entrepreneur and privy to all his affairs. The lady concerned appeared to gain no personal advantage from the significant influence she exercised over her client despite the manifest opportunities available to her! In another (and probably more common) example, it was a long-standing personal secretary. Wives (or husbands) *should* automatically fall within this class but exceptions are extremely common. The trust implicit in the confidant relationship involves not only revelation of information but also commentary on it. It may be that the entrepreneur's sense of consideration for his wife restricts him from worrying her with his business problems; or it may be that the very closeness of the personal relationship precludes objectivity in business matters.

In many cases, the confidant is someone who can be relied on but is seen to have no competitive or predatory motives. An old school friend, a retired businessman, a professional adviser or a successful executive in a wholly unrelated activity may each meet these criteria. The loyalty which the entrepreneur displays to his confidant can be as absolute as and quite contrary to his apparent distrust of everyone else. Such relationships are often very long-lasting and have their roots early in the entrepreneur's career. While distrust of the world at large is generally an unappealing attribute, it has its compensations. A trusted friend and adviser, serving the entrepreneur over many years, sharing his successes and failures, can make up for a galaxy of unsatisfactory short-term relationships.

Non-team playing

When carried to extremes, a sense of distrust of others can bring the entrepreneur problems in addition to loneliness and an unhappy personal life. It can, and does, bring enormous inefficiencies in the way in which businesses are organised and managed. The benefits which flow from powerful individualism can have opposite (and sometimes equal) penalties in terms of destroying teamwork.

When and why is teamwork important? Like many business concepts the element of teamwork needed in achieving a particular business goal varies dramatically according to the complexity of the situation. Take for example two extremes:

Johnny (ten years old) discovers that he can buy sherbert in bulk at a local cash-and-carry warehouse, split it into 50 gm bags and sell it at a 400 per cent profit in the playground. His only 'team' member is his mum who provides the starter capital for the sherbert and the paper bags. Sole trader Johnny soon achieves financial independence and relies on no one other than himself. As his own boss he can decide what to sell, how much to sell, how much to charge and so on entirely at his own discretion. The archetypal youthful millionaire in the making!

At the other extreme, NASA is determined to spend $20 billion putting a man on Mars. The project extends ten years, involves hundreds of main contractors, thousands of sub-contractors and tens of thousands of component and service suppliers. While the scientific and engineering concepts of the project require innovation and experimenta-tion its execution demands order, precision and reliability of quality and delivery. The scope for entrepreneurial flair and management eccentricity is limited to say the least, and effective teamwork between countries, companies and managers is of paramount importance.

Recognising that virtually all entrepreneurial activity lies between these extremes, the relationship between growth and the potential for entrepreneurial inefficiency caused by 'non-team' work is illustrated in the chart opposite.

The vertical axis measures teamwork capability against typical stages of organisational growth measured along the horizontal axis.

The hard line shows how teamwork becomes an increasingly dominant need, not only in terms of complexity but also of professionalism. Depending on the industry concerned, complex organisation structures (and the developing need for real specialisation) tend to emerge when more than one operating site is involved. As new activities (such as diversification away from a core business or significant addition to a product range) are added, control and management need to be more highly organised if a consistently acceptable result is to be achieved. These requirements are self-evident. The more interesting line is the jagged one which, with the hard line, defines the sector of inefficiency resulting from the involvement of the *unchanged* entrepreneur.

The jagged line shows that an entrepreneur is an effective manager when the team is small because his enthusiasm and

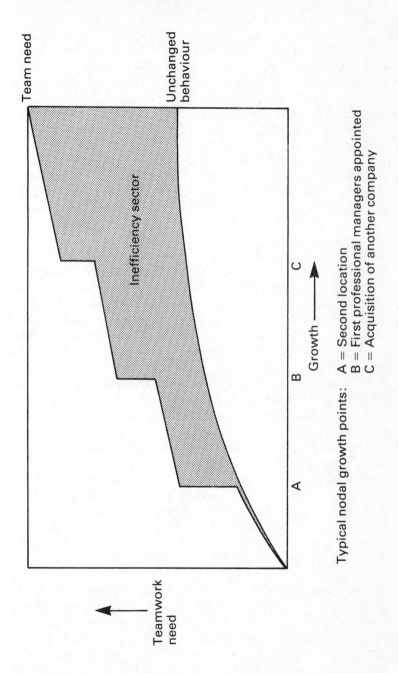

Typical nodal growth points: A = Second location
                              B = First professional managers appointed
                              C = Acquisition of another company

leadership skills are transmitted well through short lines of communication. His colleagues work within this 'aura', act flexibly, accept his idiosyncratic style without difficulty and share a powerful vision of what the organisation seeks to achieve. This missionary zeal can infect a small number of locations and a limited range of activities without any significant loss of efficiency. Successful professionals working in this environment tend to share some of the entrepreneur's anti-bureaucratic bias and consequently more readily accept the informality and lack of systems inherent in the decision-taking process. It is worth noting that the selection of these characteristics in the first professionals to join an entrepreneur is absolutely vital if a later process of acceptance of change is to follow. If the professional appointed is too rigid or systems-orientated the mutual frustration felt by him and the entrepreneur can often lead to the development of a very unsatisfactory relationship. If it subsequently fails altogether, the entrepreneur is quite likely to claim: 'I hired a qualified engineer (accountant, designer, computer expert, etc) once – it was a disaster! I'll never make the same mistake again!' The experience encourages him to resist the appointment of another professional, however pressing and obvious the need may become as the business grows. Many potentially very successful businesses are condemned to remain small as a result of this factor alone.

As the lines of communication with the entrepreneur become longer and the need for greater formality in the management process increases, the adverse effect on efficiency of an unchanged style also increases. The problem is simple: the entrepreneur must have regular and personal contact to reinforce his influence. When absent the opportunities for gossip, rumour and criticism abound. He is therefore faced either with the Herculean task of regularly seeing, and being seen by, a wider and wider group of people or increasing the intensity of his occasional contacts. The latter approach usually involves powerfully articulated instructions (or sales messages) with a minimum of persuasion. For example, the owner visits the outlying subsidiary for two hours, looks over the factory, makes instant policy decisions, gives a wide variety of instructions and departs for another three months. The effects soon wear off and he seldom finds the desired result on his next visit. He then either tries again or sacks a few people to set an example to the others! Either way, he needs compliant and willing subordinates if he is going to get away with this method. High quality managers are unlikely to be attracted to or retained by companies which operate in this way.

The root cause of these problems, and of the widening inefficiency sector as the business grows, is the unwillingness of the entrepreneur to give any real authority to anyone else. Such sharing of authority and responsibility is essential for any team effort. Entrepreneurs often feel uncomfortable in teams, always wanting to lead whatever their degree of competence, and are quite capable of employing spoiling tactics if the team effort seems to be gaining too much prominence.

These characteristics are those of the unchanged entrepreneur who is often destined to enjoy a limited local stardom. The changed entrepreneur follows the line of need and hence enjoys the efficiencies of the large corporation as well as the imagination and drive of their smaller and more innovative competitors. How is it done?

The making of the team-player

There are three components in this process of change. They can be summarised as:

1. organisational awareness;
2. judgements about people; and
3. self-management.

Each element has a vital role to play and all three are needed if the change is to succeed.

Organisational awareness
The entrepreneur has to learn and consistently follow the organisational 'shape' which suits him best. For example, Richard Branson insists that all his ventures are organised into small units with only a handful of senior people involved. Other entrepreneurs are more comfortable when dealing with only one individual in each major business (the entrepreneurial 'echo') irrespective of how big that business is. The roles of those who make commercial decisions and those who provide technical support must be sorted out in the entrepreneur's mind and a formula developed and followed. This applies, too, to the distinction between *policies* and *executive action* and level of authority appropriate for different people. It does not actually matter what the organisational format is so long as:

- it works for the entrepreneur; and
- it is consistently followed.

Organisational awareness is therefore partly an intellectual process of enquiry and analysis into what works best and partly the application of a degree of self-discipline to ensure that rules are followed. Experience constantly reminds one that people are more concerned about certainty than about the absolutes of the regime itself. In essence, it is better to know that you will be given one square meal a day than never to know whether or when you will be feasted or starved.

People judgements

The second element is the conscious recognition by the entrepreneur that he must employ neither clones nor yes-men, but people of real competence and character. This may seem self-evident but the startlingly high levels of management staff turnover in many growing entrepreneurial businesses are testament to the extent to which this is a problem. In making this change, entrepreneurs often need a lot of help, not least because they tend to be very bad interviewers. Being quick-witted and decisive people themselves, they often judge the suitability of a candidate in the first minute of an interview. For the rest of the allocated hour the interviewer will talk enthusiastically about the business while the candidate nods and murmurs occasional assent. 'An excellent candidate,' will be the entrepreneur's conclusion, despite his having collected no real data beyond the first spontaneous impression!

As businesses grow, so does the significance of some appointments in terms of business success or failure. Casual judgements are not only careless – they are particularly dangerous. The changing entrepreneur not only recognises this but is willing to accept advice and counsel on the processes involved.

Self-management

The most important change of all relates to a willingness on the part of the entrepreneur to reorganise his personal lifestyle. One of the greatest benefits of being your own boss is the freedom it offers the individual to do what he likes with his day. All entrepreneurs quickly realise that this is a limited freedom; the demands of the business are such that constant and effective attention to it are essential. As capable subordinates join the enterprise the pressure eases and the potential for variety increases. Days can be spent on a golf course, exploring a business deal or back in the office working over decisions with colleagues. The income level enjoyed by the successful man reinforces this freedom and inevitably there is a temptation for him to organise his life to suit himself and no one else.

Many small businesses are very efficiently and successfully managed on this basis. They offer a wholly satisfying life to the owners in terms of income and job satisfaction. They reflect their chosen lifestyles and make an invaluable contribution to the economy. Whether or not the owners recognise the choices they have made must be a matter of speculation. The demonstrable fact is that few, in practice, are willing and able to make the transition that is needed to the more ordered and organised life that is a prerequisite of sustained longer-term growth.

The self-disciplined entrepreneur recognises the need for the following:

- personal time management – the thoughtful apportionment of time to the various available activities;

- systematic communication with key individuals, whether the group is small or large, on a sufficiently frequent basis to encourage efficient operations;

- reliability of behaviour, allowing always for the needs of a special opportunity or crisis, so that a methodical approach is supported rather than sabotaged;

- moderation of style – difficult for many – involving the acceptance that documentation, formality, debate and monitoring are all necessary parts of running a successful enterprise.

There is nothing here that will surprise any experienced business executive. What it represents for the fast-moving entrepreneur, however, is often an insuperable hurdle. Professional advisers frequently have a crucial, catalytic, role to play in ensuring that the change is made with as much emphasis on the benefits (and conversely as little on the pain) as possible. Making money consistently and long term over a widening horizon of interests may seem easy to the entrepreneur convinced of his own abilities. In truth, it needs organisation, good people and self-discipline. The entrepreneur must grasp and deliver each if he is to succeed.

I know best!

The process of learning to be a team-player can, and sometimes does, lead the previously successful entrepreneur down a dangerous path towards equivocation and indecision. Everyone knows the old definition of a committee as 'a cul-de-sac into which ideas are lured and quietly done to death'. The single-mindedness of the leader can equally be subject to the destructive forces of debate if they are allowed to get out of hand.

The need to delegate, consult and take expert counsel must be tempered by a degree of self-confidence which at its simplest, can be expressed as 'I know best!' In some cases this manifests itself in a willingness to override the most compelling and logical of counter-arguments – to go out on a limb and to quell adverse comment. It is perhaps the most central indication of the entrepreneur at work that he will, when convinced of the rightness of his case, follow his own judgement whatever the strength of the counter-arguments.

By saying 'I know best', the entrepreneur not only personally embraces the inherent risk of failure but also the loyalty and support of those around him. To ignore sensible advice and logical argument simply out of bravado is, of course, a sure road to failure. To assess the risks and opportunities differently from those around you and make a decision based on 'gut feeling' is quite different. A practical example will illustrate the distinction.

A successful operator of used car lots decides to expand his business into a major new urban centre. The market analysis and competitor information he obtains, backed by the calculations made by his accountant, suggest that the available payback in the new territory is small and the risk of failure considerable. The forecasts suggest that not only will the market be hard to break into but offers little in terms of satisfactory long-term results. The owner decides to go ahead anyway, and after months of hard work and losses decides to close down the new outlet. The reasons for the failure were exactly those described in the initial analysis: the operator failed to find any new 'angle' or exploitable opportunity which would prove that analysis fallacious. The process of being proved right no doubt pleased the professionals but was costly in terms of both finance and reputation to the entrepreneur himself.

Contrast this case with that of a manufacturer bringing a new form of packaging material to the grocery trade. Experimental operations have demonstrated the superior qualities of the new material and its potentially very advantageous cost characteristics. There is only one snag – the plant needed to manufacture significant volumes requires a very large capital investment and the payback is highly speculative in view of the novelty of the material. Conventional analysis, based on the rate of uptake of comparable new products, suggests that the risks are unacceptably high and rejection of the project or, at best, a joint venture with a major corporation is universally recommended. The entrepreneur says 'I know best' and presses on to bring the project to a startlingly successful launch and equally profitable further development phase.

Why was this a different result from the earlier example? The reason is that the first entrepreneur failed to find any new way to sell motor cars; the second, by contrast, showed a special insight into the behaviour of manufacturers of grocery products. He realised that the attraction of the packaging material to the manufacturer lay not only in its lower cost but in its ability to display the product more effectively on the shelf. This intangible benefit was 'felt' by the promoter of the project rather than measured in any conventional way. In prospect, he saw this factor in terms of specific levels of sales and manufacturing throughput which made him more inherently optimistic than any of the forecasts. More optimistic but not groundlessly so – hence the key difference between the examples.

Many of these moments of judgement are as instinctive and difficult to analyse as the ones described above although a 'hunch' or 'feel' are seldom as irrational as they might at first appear. Many entrepreneurs claim to rely on little else although, in truth, the combination of shrewd observation, fine judgement of risk and a facility with numbers is seldom easy to describe. An entrepreneur unable (or unwilling) to make controversial decisions is likely to be a long-term loser. He is allowed and expected to make mistakes and many would argue that, without failure, the individual is ill-prepared to achieve long-term success. Clearly, the stronger the track record the more robust the capability to sustain a particular setback, whether as a result of an 'I know best' decision or a fully supported analysis. The most valuable insight an entrepreneur can have, however, is the ability to know just why he contradicts opposing advice when his decision ultimately proves the right one. Armed with that knowledge, he should be able to go anywhere!

Summary

The entrepreneur is an easily recognisable and undoubted individualist. The distinctive characteristics are an invariable propensity to rebel and an impatience with the conventional. Although various theories have been advanced to explain this, the underlying reason is likely to be his desire for recognition and 'applause'.

As a non-joiner the entrepreneur rarely makes a good team member. Although this is potentially an advantage when a business is small, it increasingly affects efficiency as it grows. If the entrepreneur is unwilling or unable to change it can determine the scope for growth more certainly than any other factor. To achieve the change from a non-team player to a team-player he needs to learn new skills and attitudes, not least in terms of how he organises his own business life.

An entrepreneur must be able to stamp his authority on key decisions even if his view appears to fly in the face of logical analysis and advice. The 'hunch' factor is often based on clear, but subconscious, processes which are extremely valid in relation to the commercial argument. The entrepreneur who can rationalise this capability and turn it to work for him has a remarkable and powerful tool at his command.

Chapter 5

Manager

A crucial element in the make-up of the successful entrepreneur, in addition to his being an innovator and a risk-taker, is his role as a manager. The management process he uses is usually very different from that normally associated with established businesses. In this chapter we explore some of the characteristics of the entrepreneur in performing the essential tasks needed to follow through from the inception of the business idea to its realisation as a profitable enterprise.

Opportunist or planner?

The following table is drawn from an article in the March–April 1985 edition of the *Harvard Business Review*. In that article ('The Heart of Entrepreneurship') Howard Stevenson and David Gumpert drew a series of contrasting pictures of the entrepreneurial versus the administrative culture. The table overleaf summarises the characteristics and pressures of the extremes of an entrepreneurial focus and an administrative focus. Its significance for the entrepreneur lies in the insight it offers into the management culture in which they thrive compared with those dedicated to more bureaucratic objectives.

Each of the cultural dimensions is worth a brief commentary.

Strategic vision
The entrepreneur feels the pressure of a changing world and the need to grasp opportunities by the scruff of the neck. The bureaucrat, by contrast, feels the pressure to demonstrate his control of his business environment and sees this as a desirable strategic objective. Thus the two see the world in a totally different light: the entrepreneur sees energetic exploitation as a desirable goal while the bureaucrat is cautious and conservative. This analysis

The entepreneurial culture *v* the administrative culture

Entrepreneurial focus

	Characteristics	Pressures
A Strategic orientation	Driven by perception of opportunity	Diminishing opportunities Rapidly changing technology, consumer economics, social values and political rules
B Commitment to seize opportunities	Revolutionary, with short duration	Action orientation Narrow decision windows Acceptance of reasonable risks Few decision constituencies
C Commitment of resources	Many stages, with minimal exposure at each stage	Lack of predictable resource needs Lack of control over the environment Social demands for appropriate use of resources Foreign competition Demands for more efficient resource use
D Control of resources	Episodic use or rent of required resources	Increased resource specialisation Long resource life compared with need Risk of obsolescence Risk inherent in the identified opportunity Inflexibility of permanent commitment to resources
E Management structure	Flat, with multiple informal networks	Coordination of key non-controlled resources Challenge to hierarchy Employees' desire for independence

Administrative focus

Characteristics	Pressures
Driven by controlled resources	Social contracts
	Performance measurement criteria
	Planning systems and cycles
Evolutionary, with long duration	Acknowledgement of multiple constituencies
	Negotiation about strategic course
	Risk reduction
	Coordination with existing resource base
A single stage, with complete commitment out of decision	Need to reduce risk
	Incentive compensation
	Turnover in managers
	Capital budgeting systems
	Formal planning systems
Ownership or employment of required resources	Power, status and financial rewards
	Coordination of activity
	Efficiency measures
	Inertia and cost of change
	Industry structures
Hierarchy	Need for clearly defined authority and responsibility
	Organisational culture
	Reward systems
	Management theory

also suggests that there is a time pressure on the entrepreneur evidenced by a feeling that unless he acts quickly the window of opportunity will close. Bureaucrats, by contrast, are more concerned with method than with output and assume a relatively unchanged external environment.

Seizing opportunities

The entrepreneur wants to get on with the job and his actions are decision-orientated. He therefore consults few people in the process and relies strongly on his own judgement. The administrator, by contrast, uses more incremental processes based on wider consultation and negotiation. He is aware of the existing situation and seeks to amend and develop it without involving radical change. Once again, the entrepreneur is more aware of time pressure than his bureaucratic counterpart.

Resource commitment

The pressures illustrated as applying to the entrepreneur have in common a rather chaotic state of interacting forces, with the entrepreneur sitting at the centre. His approach is eclectic, consisting of picking off each element of the equation and dealing with it individually. By contrast, the administrator sees the need for a homogeneous pattern of interlocking systems and methods which will integrate with decision-taking processes. These show a clear contrast between recognition of a chaotic world from which order can seldom be expected on the one hand, and an ordered world in which chaos is an aberration on the other. The entrepreneur often seeks to exploit chaos while the bureaucrat strives to bring it into order. This analysis of extremes does not bring out the fact that the entrepreneur's approach to resource commitment is usually no less systematic than that of the administrator; it simply has a different point of departure in terms of the assumptions made about the environment in which each must work.

Resource control

The entrepreneurial focus is on an opportunistically driven commitment to resources, to the point of a careless lack of concern for the longer term. By contrast, the bureaucrat is anxiously concerned for the efficiency and coordination of resources and is deeply conscious of their long-term effectiveness. This suggests that the entrepreneur is more interested in the *output* of the process, namely profit, than in the means of achieving it. 'Control' as an activity is, therefore, inherently uninteresting unless it has a very direct and evident bearing on the outcome of the venture.

Management structure

The entrepreneur classically uses very informal and direct lines of management in the control of his business activities. By contrast, the administrator seeks clarity of organisation and hierarchy as a means of achieving control over the enterprise. The entrepreneur therefore acts to harness management effort towards the achievement of a well-articulated and common goal whereas the bureaucrat seeks to make the individual the servant of the system.

The two models described in the table represent extreme but readily recognisable descriptions of the way entrepreneurs, as distinct from bureaucrats, behave. Both styles of management are valid and effective in their respective environments. It is important, however, to recognise that the entrepreneur manages his business in a very different way from his opposite number in a more conventional and mature organisation. Thus he is likely to be more concerned with the achievement of short-term objectives, more profligate with resources, and less sensitive to the need for structure and consultation than his more professionally trained colleague. This can be illustrated by a real life example.

———— ◊ ————

A successful businessman, Harry Wren, runs three clothing factories making ladies' fashion garments. The three factories are within ten miles of one another and employ some 150 full-time staff plus 300 part-time outworkers. One factory manufactures skirts, another jackets and boleros and the third trousers and culottes. Harry manages the factories through a constant round of personal supervision at each location which he combines with visiting major customers, choosing each season's designs and buying key raw materials. His investment in equipment is substantial and he prides himself on the efficiency of his manufacturing facilities.

One day he is approached by a potential major customer. This large chain of retailers has grown dissatisfied with their existing supplier and is contemplating a change. The total order they could offer Harry would represent 80 per cent of his annual output but would involve scrapping a major part of his existing plant. His business would become 'tied' to one customer although the opportunity for long-term profit looks very attractive.

Harry conceives the notion that he can exploit this business opportunity by combining two of his existing units and adding a major new production facility all of which would be located on an out-of-town site. This project involves a considerable gamble in terms of loss of production continuity, the willingness of his labour force to relocate and the potential payback on a substantial investment in new plant. Harry's exercise in planning involves a relatively optimistic view of each of these factors. He is sanguine about his capability to serve his new customer long term and, indeed, expand the business further on the basis of that connection.

In the event Harry's plan foundered through lack of appreciation of the practical difficulties involved in making a complex change to his business. The individualistic, hands-on style which had proved so successful was quite inadequate to cope with the logistics of a major operation. His management and planning processes were too weak to avoid a disastrous failure in producing the quantities and quality required. In consequence, Harry was left with a major investment burden and a very dissatisfied customer, waiting for the first opportunity to move elsewhere. Harry then had little option but to retrench and adopt more conventional management processes to help him out of his difficulty.

There are many illustrations of how the informality and opportunism of the entrepreneur contribute to the successful early growth of young organisations. In these early phases the entrepreneur not only has an encyclopaedic knowledge of his business and all that goes on in it, but a keenness to attend to detail which in some cases verges on the paranoic. Such individuals have been known to fly into a rage if some small aspect of a sales presentation or a letter fails to meet his personal quality expectations. A misplaced desk in an office, an untidy showroom or a badly typed address on a letter can each offend the entrepreneur's perfectionism. The instant dismissal of a badly dressed clerk by a bad-tempered entrepreneur is certainly not unknown.

This understanding of the business and attention to detail weakens as the business grows. The entrepreneur attempts to compensate by both working harder and relying on spot checks. His grasp of details of the company's affairs inexorably weakens and in consequence he must rely increasingly on the work of his managers and subordinates. They have been used to a boss with a total grasp of the business and have probably had little authority or decision-taking responsibility. The owner's need to delegate may therefore not find a response in the capability of his subordinates. They may have become too set in their ways to change or simply lack the talent to grow with the business. For the reasons described earlier in this chapter the entrepreneur is sometimes the last person to introduce and manage essential new systems and as a result the growth process slows and ultimately stops.

A well-organised entrepreneur recognises that he faces a series of watershed decision points at which his willingness to adjust the focus of the organisation is called into question.

Typical watershed decision points

There are a number of these inherent in the growth of most entrepreneurial businesses. The following are some illustrations:

- the need for costing and management reporting systems other than the cash book or the back of the entrepreneur's personal envelope;
- the need to define the job responsibilities of senior colleagues and their working relationships to each other;
- the introduction, for the first time, of a senior professionally trained manager;
- the need to be accountable to some third party, such as a minority shareholder or banker;
- becoming involved in a joint venture or trading for the first time overseas;
- the acquisition of another company, particularly when it trades in a different location or product range.

The 'correct' response at these decision points will inevitably vary depending on the particular circumstances of the company in terms of size, profitability and business sector. There will however always be a need to move towards formality and a more systematic method of management. The challenge for the entrepreneur is to adapt to these needs without sacrificing the essential qualities which have made his business successful up to that time.

Retaining the good qualities

The paradox of the managerial behaviour of the entrepreneur is the apparent ease with which a careless disregard for conventional management methods is often combined with extraordinary efficiency of operation. There can be no doubt that the 'task' orientation of a small business can give it a distinct competitive advantage over its more hierarchically structured and ponderous competitors. The boundaries which normally exist between separate jobs disappear in a strongly motivated small team. The catalytic effect of a focused and energetic owner serves to encourage people both to care about their working responsibilities and to perform above their normal potentiality. The adrenalin charge which accompanies a high risk business venture is perhaps akin to that experienced by the soldier in combat. The entrepreneur both understands and exploits this emotional drive.

In conditions of aggressive leadership the entrepreneur's judgement and instructions are seldom questioned. For example, if he takes extraordinary steps to check on the fine details of subordinates' actions it is likely to be interpreted as caring for the overall performance of the enterprise as much as unwelcome interference in it. One owner of a successful engineering company saw every incoming and outgoing piece of correspondence, even when the annual turnover amounted to £20 million. Another insisted on personally checking the layout of every branch office in a national network and adjusting the seating arrangements to his personal taste. A successful business owner who personally checks every employee's expense claim is not uncommon.

This very personal and involved style is frequently combined with an unconventional approach to business management. Some typical traits of behaviour are:

- great impatience with any sort of formal meeting;
- a dislike of routine as exemplified by regular management information in all its forms;
- an unwillingness to define individuals' roles with particular clarity or to treat them consistently;
- demonstrating his command of the decision-taking structure by periodically upsetting it without apparent cause.

It would be foolish to suggest that many successful entrepreneurs do not develop into highly capable managers. However they often seem to retain some, if not all, of the characteristics listed above, if only in a more muted and controlled form.

A management style which has a shifting focus depending on the most pressing issue of the day has some distinct advantages. Thus the entrepreneur who brings to his boardroom a particular concern for intensive debate and discussion, sweeping aside the normal agenda, may achieve more than is possible in the structured environment of a larger company. For example, if the owner gets a bee in his bonnet about selling the company's product in the United States he might introduce it unheralded at a board meeting and insist on its being fully debated there and then. This often irritates and frustrates functionally responsible directors who would have preferred thinking and preparation time before making a reasoned submission. The element of surprise, however, often leads to more successful brainstorming than weeks of careful preparation. Many entrepreneurs consciously employ this tactic to develop an important issue without being pressed to make a particular decision; it often adds to their capability of acting quickly and opportunistically. The difficulty which experienced executives have in adapting to this style of environment should not, however, be underrated. A sales or finance director joining a rapidly growing company from a larger enterprise will often find this highly volatile management approach very difficult to cope with. As one senior director put it, 'It's like a combination of a roller coaster and the tunnel of love. It is enormously exciting and confusing at one and the same time. I quickly gave up trying to find my organisational bearings and let myself be swept along by the tide of the company's enthusiasm.'

Non-planning

Since the essence of entrepreneurship is the quickness of wit to seize commercial opportunities and to innovate, it is, theoretically at least, counter to the planning ethic. As discussed earlier, entrepreneurs can demonstrate considerable accomplishment when it comes to planning where the persuasion of others is the prime purpose. Thus the fund-raising stage in any major venture must involve a considerable degree of care in preparing forecasts if it is to prove successful. This style of planning which attempts to describe and predict future events is much more agreeable to the entrepreneur than the formalised system used for day-to-day management purposes. Skills in the use of budgetary control and cash-flow forecasting are not those which immediately come to mind when considering the successful entrepreneur. There are, of course, notable exceptions, particularly in such fields as property development, commodity trading, international banking and finance. By and large, the entrepreneur gets bored with such mundane management tools and while he is fully prepared to allow others to employ them if they wish, seldom feels the obligation to be constrained by them himself.

Presenting a business proposition to an entrepreneur equally requires special skills. The concept, the market opportunity and the vision of what can be achieved are as important as the detailed financial projections. The overall result must, of course, be clearly explained and risks and return closely argued. Adding a venture to the portfolio of an entrepreneur is a more subtle process than simply offering him a money-making opportunity. The venture has implications for his personal standing, his business power base and the opportunities for future leverage. These must be taken fully into account when judging the likely reaction to what may seem a particularly attractive deal.

A sound judge of men

The non-planning entrepreneur must of necessity rely very heavily on the support and energy of his management team. As businesses develop and grow, his reliance on such individuals increases enormously. He must therefore:

- choose them carefully;
- use them effectively; and
- maintain the strength of the team.

Successful choices

Choosing able lieutenants, particularly when they operate in specialised areas, is a very difficult job for the inexperienced businessman. He tends to look for a combination of personal and professional qualities which are often very difficult to find, particularly in those who are willing to take the chance of working for a strong-minded and wilful boss. The personal qualities seem to require a subordinate to be strong and independent-minded but only to the point at which compliance with the ultimate decision of the entrepreneur is both accepted and implemented. It is flattering to the entrepreneur to engage in stimulating internal debate with the confident knowledge that his final judgement will prevail. Many with a modest educational background seek out those with some academic distinction and take pride in the reflected glory of their achievement. In reality the employee, if he survives, comes to recognise the nature of the trade-off and seeks compensation for it through the salary or dividend cheque. Entrepreneurs prefer their colleagues to be good listeners and to be able to conjure up the necessary enthusiasm for the company mission. They are expected to be loyal and not prone to conspiracy; they are also assumed to be willing to give little priority to their private lives when the demands of the company dictate otherwise.

In technical disciplines, the entrepreneur is often on much weaker ground. He may find it extremely difficult to judge the competence of an individual despite an apparently lustrous track record. The informality of the management style often means that an individual's inadequacy takes a long time to be revealed. The appointment of the very first finance director, for example, may attract to a company an individual with a wholly unsuitable background. He may be more interested in doing deals with the owner than in managing a well-organised accounts department. The entrepreneur's lack of technical understanding of the issues involved along with no formal system of review may leave this problem unappreciated until some collapse occurs. Similar examples would apply in the manufacturing and technical areas of a business, although the entrepreneur usually has a better understanding of products and processes than he does of finance. Some managers undoubtedly enjoy the freedom and informality of the less strictly structured entrepreneurial business environment; they can be both more creative and influential in its development. It is also a more precarious position to be in.

Effective man management

Typically, the entrepreneur communicates with his managers orally rather than in writing and with no particular, regular agenda. The communication process is therefore characterised by an untidy mélange of major and minor items handled in no ordered sequence of logic or priority. The sales director, for example, might speak to his boss four times in the course of a day. The issues might be:

- pricing a major new contract for which a tender is due to be submitted;
- a complaint about late delivery from a customer whom the owner has met casually at lunch-time;
- sales commission scales for the coming year; and
- a hotel bill for a salesman's stay abroad, attached to a cheque requiring the owner's signature.

This typical kaleidoscopic pattern of day-to-day interchange involves little in the form of direct instruction or formal performance review and monitoring. The executive must use each contact with the owner as another small piece of evidence in the jigsaw of his job role. This may itself represent a moving picture as the entrepreneur explores the boundaries of his subordinate's contribution to the business.

Few entrepreneurs comply with the common image of the autocrat barking instructions down the phone to his trembling subordinate. The style is much more likely to be indirect and persuasive, particularly when senior colleagues are involved. For example, one most feared entrepreneur never seemed to give a direct instruction. He would say, 'George, I suggest you check out the results of the Amsterdam branch' or 'I was wondering, Frank, if the sales figures for the last quarter really came up to your expectations' and so on. The message behind the innocent comment or question was entirely clear to his colleagues and energetic action invariably followed.

The utterances of some entrepreneurs are more Delphic and are probably aimed at keeping the management team on their toes. Thus an entrepreneur might comment to his board, 'I'm pretty unhappy about the way our business is organised' without any further explanation. The effect on individuals can, of course, be galvanising since no one is sure at whom the remark is directed. Another technique is the so-called 'confidential briefing' of one colleague about another with a high degree of certainty that the information will leak to the person about whom the comment is made. Demanding, and usually receiving, considerable personal loyalty from his subordinates does not always earn the corresponding response from the entrepreneur: as companies grow, the business management team forms 'clusters' of professionalism at some remove from the influence of the entrepreneur himself. They may be very formally structured, as would be the case in a conventional company owned at arm's length by a successful man. Part of that function is to 'translate' and, on occasion, rationalise the entrepreneur's decisions. The owner would communicate with the managing director and perhaps one or two others at board level and they would be subject to his particular style, however idiosyncratic. However, lower levels of operational management would be insulated from this influence.

Despite these apparent flaws, entrepreneurs are frequently very skilful in wresting high-level performance out of their immediate subordinates. The word 'charisma' is often used to describe the special quality which these natural leaders possess. It is difficult to describe in simple terms but is often instantly recognisable when someone who possesses it enters the room. It is partly the reputation of the individual which is subconsciously transmitted to those around him; it is also partly the exceptional commitment and energy which some people bring to all their activities. This yields an almost involuntary recognition in most of us and goes some way to explaining why the professional manager is often willing to work in what others might regard as very unsatisfactory business circumstances.

A healthy team

Entrepreneurs are commonly seen to be, and indeed are, extremely ruthless when it comes to dealing with individuals. Issues of fairness are often subordinated to the interest of the enterprise or the entrepreneur himself. In many cases, the attitude towards an individual colleague is less than wholly rational and the more senior his position the more vulnerable he is likely to be. Typical causes of an unheralded dismissal at this level include:

- suspicion of disloyalty or conspiracy;
- a fall from favour, perhaps over some apparently trifling point or issue;
- a major confrontation which goes beyond the boundaries of the unwritten protocol between the two individuals; and
- boredom and a wish for change.

These reasons may appear facile at first glance but must be taken seriously by the senior executive who values the security of his position. Conventional assumptions about the gentlemanly conduct of one individual to another, particularly when the association is a long-standing one, tend to prove unreliable. The entrepreneur's actions are often sudden and brutal, but financially generous. It seems almost as if his mind can flick over from a lively and highly personal association one day to a cold independence the next; the actions are justified by what is seen to be the better interest of the business itself. A reputation for being decisive in handling people can be an entrepreneur's strong card and the occasional senior management dismissal can *'encourage les autres'*. In private, the entrepreneur often finds the process both distasteful and difficult and suffers many of the anxieties which would be expected of more feeling individuals. These anxieties are never displayed in public for much the same reason that a successful military commander would not reveal to his troops his doubts about the potential success of a campaign. In many cases the 'hard but fair' philosophy of man management is a valuable component in the entrepreneurial style.

Many large companies suffer from a reluctance to take difficult man management decisions. They often tend to dodge the issue either by compromising the process of judgement itself or shying away from the unpleasantness of a personal confrontation. The shake-out in British industry in the early 1980s hardened many managers' attitudes towards this problem. Despite this, there is still a general tendency for companies as they grow to become increasingly bureaucratic and impersonal, with a resultant blurring of the sharp edges of personal assessment which is so important a skill for the entrepreneur.

Healthy teams exist in all types of organisations. They are often, however, no more than a fleeting phenomenon and it requires a firm hand and keen judgement to maintain their effectiveness. Military history indicates the frequency with which generals need to change their command teams for continued success in the field. The analogy applies equally well to the business world. Using the military parallel, the entrepreneur has an understanding of the objectives of the campaign and consequently thinks little of the changes he needs to make in his senior team to achieve success. Some large organisations are sufficiently astute to recognise the need constantly to reiterate such a strategic vision. They rarely succeed in maintaining a healthy team, however, unless they are prepared to apply a similar degree of entrepreneurial ruthlessness to it.

The ethics of management

It is often argued that entrepreneurs find it difficult to distinguish between management behaviour which is generally acceptable (or 'ethical') and that which falls into a more dubious category. The interesting issue here is not one of the entrepreneur acting illegally (for which there are clear risks and penalties); it is rather the question of why such people are so commonly assumed to act in a relatively underhand way and whether this assumption is borne out by general experience.

Given that entrepreneurs are frequently unconventional and untrained, at least in the early stages of their careers, it is hardly surprising that they do not conform to common management stereotypes. Someone working with an entrepreneur is likely to see only a fraction of his total working methods. As entrepreneurs are individualistic, and often secretive in their approach, this 'glimpse' of how the boss works can be disturbing for more conventionally trained managers. Decision-making can appear sporadic and partial if not occasionally contradictory, and since the entrepreneur collects data from many sources but often keeps his own counsel, his methods can give rise to suspicions of conspiracy. However much his success is recognised and applauded, his motives may be questioned. His attempts to communicate and explain his actions frequently create the reverse of the desired effect among his colleagues. Thus the wish to rationalise and explain a process which is essentially somewhat arcane does no more than ring new alarm bells.

All these factors tend to create an atmosphere in which assumptions of deviousness flourish. These are further reinforced by typical questions about what rules are normal and how far they can be broken within the boundaries of legality. Accountants and lawyers are very familiar with such questions from their entrepreneurial clients. For example, an entrepreneur in the process of bidding for a private company owned by a widely spread family may ask how far it is usual to approach distant relatives at the same time as dealing with the major shareholder. He might be told that such a method is legal but generally regarded as unethical since such negotiations are dealt with through principal shareholders whose views are respected in such situations. The entrepreneur may or may not seek to ignore the ethical rules, but by asking the question he is showing an inclination to be, at best, unconventional in his methods.

It can be argued that the entrepreneur is a valuable catalyst in the process of change, continually throwing down challenges to the conventional order. When Sir Charles Clore of the British Shoe Corporation first started the process of buying and breaking up companies in the 1960s, his activities were regarded as deeply shocking by the financial world. Such behaviour was seen as unacceptable by those brought up to expect a more gentlemanly way of doing business. However, it did not take long for the financial world to realise and accept the commanding underlying logic of the Clore method. What was seen initially as a maverick approach became commonplace in later years. It is interesting to see how today's 'corporate raiders' are retracing the path trodden by such original entrepreneurial minds some 30 years ago.

It is equally true to suppose that the entrepreneur feels driven by his ambition to succeed and make money to adopt whatever techniques are legally available to him. This propensity to seek a competitive advantage at any cost often makes such individuals, in prospect at least, unattractive business associates. The reputation for sharp practice often precedes that of business achievement; it has undesirable overtones and creates an atmosphere of suspicion and distrust.

In many cases, this assumption that entrepreneurs invariably sail close to the wind is quite unfounded. Being a quick and ruthless decision-taker does not necessarily mean that rules have to be broken and a strong sense of personal ambition does not necessarily imply that the means will justify the end. In practice, there seems to be a greater likelihood of the successful entrepreneur's acting unconventionally than unethically. A case history illustrates this point.

A strongly lead software house is desperately keen to win a major systems development contract. The customer is a major public corporation and competitors for the work have apparently much stronger credentials in terms of previous relevant experience. Within the confines of legality the software house can act unethically or unconventionally. In the former category would fall, for example, head-hunting staff from competitor firms and hoping to obtain information on the rival bids during the interview process; in the latter would be creative and unusual sales techniques – for example, arranging a surprise personal demonstration of their software to the potential customer's chairman at his golf club would be unconventional but certainly not unethical. The software house concerned is more likely to adopt the latter approach than the former and this is true of general entrepreneurial behaviour. The entrepreneur's wish to be seen as a somewhat macho figure often encourages him to play to the audience: thus he will suggest that he has obtained some information by devious means when in reality it is available from some commonplace source. This is not to suggest that he will not exploit some loophole in law or accepted conventions, but rather that there is usually a stronger moral and ethical sense at work than popular prejudice would suggest.

Unsafe assumptions

Most businessmen and professionals rely on an unspoken but generally understood code of business practice. Their training and development lead them to make certain assumptions about the way in which others with whom they deal are likely to behave. These even extend to the minutiae of business relations, such as how people will dress, how correspondence is conducted, telephone calls answered and meetings run. Entrepreneurs quite commonly have different but consistent sets of business values. For example, some entrepreneurs dispense with what are generally regarded as the courtesies of business life: correspondence remains unanswered but meetings can be and are interrupted at his whim; colleagues and advisers are called at any time of the day or night to discuss a problem and social niceties are ignored. Everything is secondary to the immediacy of the business issue and those who work with an entrepreneur of this type must recognise and understand this priority.

Almost every entrepreneur has some idiosyncratic characteristics which make him an unconventional manager. The important message for those dealing with him is to understand his pattern of behaviour and not to make any generalised assumptions based on ordinary experience. Entrepreneurs dislike being taken for granted almost as much as they dislike being ignored.

Older and wiser?

The picture which emerges from this analysis is of the entrepreneur as a dominant and individualistic manager. He has little truck with management theory and imposes his own personal style on all his activities. In principle, this approach ought to impose severe limitations on the size of the enterprise such a person can control. This should be dictated by the degree to which he needs to understand the detailed issues in order to make effective decisions; beyond a certain point, there is simply insufficient time for him to make sound judgements and the success of the business is thus compromised. Depending on the type of business involved this boundary condition would conventionally be met when more than, say, 200 people are employed.

If this were universally true, entrepreneurs would never progress beyond the confines of the small company. Indeed, many are destined to remain leaders of such businesses simply because they cannot make the transition from a 'hands-on' style to a more professional management approach. For many, experience brings the necessary insight into the process of delegation and the need for more formal methods of management.

The entrepreneur also realises that the most secure and important resource is his own time and that it must be used wisely. The personal agenda increasingly reflects self-discipline and a more ordered approach to his dealings with his colleagues; the self-indulgence which characterises the early stages of many entrepreneurially based businesses gives way to a more conventional and ordered life. The pace and excitement may remain the same but the working structure progressively develops into a more ordered model.

Growing older and wiser may also be characterised by a more mature and measured personal style. Although there are notable exceptions to this rule, those who break through the size barrier do so, in part, by acquiring greater skills of diplomacy and professionalism. They become more reasonable, tactful and thoughtful. Their management style becomes more relaxed and considered, while remaining authoritative. In many senses, they enjoy the best of both worlds – the pleasures and wealth of the entrepreneur and the professionalism of the experienced manager.

The experience which leads some entrepreneurs but not others to realise the importance of these factors is not itself a function of age – the lessons can be learnt at a very early age and a fully-fledged 'entrepreneur–manager' can emerge in his early twenties. Such, it seems, was the case with Richard Branson whose business empire was founded and developed early on in his career. Some achieve this breakthrough much later, perhaps as a result of learning from a series of disappointments and failures or from the experience of their peers. In private business there are regular examples of entrepreneurs whose willingness to change their approach comes only with middle age.

None of the managerial characteristics described above is of any value without the essential flair and innovation which go with the entrepreneurial spirit. The sad truth is that success and the wealth and power which accompany it often blind the entrepreneur to the necessity for personal development if there are to be longer-term achievements. The learning process is less an intellectual exercise than one which follows an insight into enlightened self-interest. Entrepreneurs are often so convinced of their uniqueness that they find such insights difficult to accept. They are, however, ultimately the determinant of management success in the larger company arena.

Summary

The entrepreneur needs to succeed as a manager if he is to achieve his goal of wealth creation and power. Management through conventional processes is not usually the entrepreneur's forte; however, he brings to the task a clear and determined style which frequently achieves greater success than the more structured and measured methods used by larger companies. He is more likely to be unconventional than unethical in his approach to business but relishes the reputation of being troublesome. To succeed in building a business of real substance, he must learn to make the transition from a dominating and idiosyncratic style to one which involves more delegation and personal self-discipline. In the last analysis, the entrepreneur–manager will only succeed if he realises the imperative of recognising the contribution which others can make to this ultimate achievement.

Chapter 6

Prima Donna

The Napoleon factor

An essential part of the make-up of any leader is his capacity to command the respect of his subordinates. The personal qualities involved are not easily defined but certainly include the ability to make sound judgements about both situations and people. The skills needed to judge situations, whether at a strategic or tactical level, can be acquired by anyone with a reasonable intellectual capacity, and the armed forces and big business have demonstrated the value of investing in management training to develop their leaders, whether in the field of battle or the boardrooms in the City. The skills needed to judge people soundly, however, are much less easily taught: although certain ground rules are generally applicable, it is clear that experience is the dominant tutor.

In conventional environments, individuals with leadership qualities are nurtured through a combination of training and front-line experience. The former broadens the intellectual horizons and introduces the analytical and planning techniques needed to appraise a problem, while the latter develops the recipient's talents in the judgement of how individuals are likely to behave in differing situations. How different is this structured and progressive approach from the background experience of most entrepreneurs? Though some do, of course, emerge from backgrounds in large corporations to break away and establish new enterprises, they represent a small minority of the entrepreneurial population. Most entrepreneurs therefore emerge from backgrounds which are much less structured and hierarchical than those in which leadership skills are commonly developed. Theirs is the advantage of having an earlier, self-determined opportunity to put their leadership talents to the test; they may also have the disadvantage of lack of experience of working in a well-ordered environment which brings a different perspective to both achievements and personal standards. As already discussed, most entrepreneurs are, by their nature, non-joiners and non-conformists. Their self-belief is so strong that they set their own standards of behaviour which are frequently very different from those of the people around them. As a consequence, the entrepreneur works within his own set of standards rather than those imposed by others. The potential for him to act irrationally, unfairly or even despotically is thereby hugely increased.

These characteristics can conveniently be called the 'Napoleon factor'. Some entrepreneurs, like Napoleon, suffer from such a degree of self-delusion about their own powers that they fail to anticipate, and hence avoid, ultimate failure. They overstep the fine line between soundly judged self-confidence and reckless bravura. In extreme cases, the entrepreneur's behaviour breaks the bonds of confidence which he has so carefully established with those around him and his impending failure is signalled by a collapse of the team on whose support he could previously rely. The deserted entrepreneur is left as a rather pitiable figure proclaiming his mastery of a situation which is no longer his to command.

It seems that all entrepreneurs have the potential to cross this line and hence considerably increase the risk of failure. It is therefore instructive both to them and to those around them to be aware of the early symptoms of a possible problem. There are three critical indicators:

- The demand for loyalty;
- The uncertain temper; and
- Unreliable leadership.

The demand for loyalty
The trail-blazing entrepreneur creates loyalty through the dedication he has to his project and his ability to convert opportunity into profit. The loyalty this creates is founded perhaps more in admiration for an extraordinary talent than respect for the personal qualities of the entrepreneur. In these early stages, the entrepreneur is more likely to persuade and lead by example than by direction and command. As success is achieved the influence of the entrepreneur, particularly over his subordinates, increases rapidly and can extend far beyond what appears to an independent observer as wholly rational. This situation can be illustrated by a simple, real life example.

Freddie Jones, at 50, is a successful entrepreneur. Having founded a building company in his twenties he now owns three hotels and a travel agency and has gathered around him a professional management team including a finance director. His leisure-time passion is sailing and he can see a new business venture in the boat-building business. All his advisers, including his own management, strongly advise that it would be very unwise to go ahead with this investment. They point out the rate of business failures in that sector, the overcapacity already available in the industry and the difficulties inherent in controlling boat-building staff. Despite this advice, Freddie pursues his instinct, buys the boatyard and proceeds to invest heavily in it. The funds needed considerably exceed original estimates. Freddie has to borrow against his other investments and then, after 18 months, sell some of his assets to keep the project going. His originally cheerful forecast of a highly successful and profitable business are gradually replaced by an expectation of break-even and then loss minimisation. Ultimately, he is forced to close the boatyard, make the staff redundant and sell the stock for whatever it will realise.

This sad episode extends over a total period of three years. The enterprise was entirely at the risk of Freddie himself and this was recognised by his boardroom colleagues. After the initial commitment was made, however, Freddie would not permit any of them, at any time, to make comments suggesting that the original judgement was at fault. The problems and the loss-making were attributed to 'the market' or 'labour relations' or 'poor on-site management'. He expected, and got, an extraordinary degree of public loyalty from his colleagues. In private, of course, they were endlessly critical of the decision and the absurd tenaciousness with which Freddie followed it through. His demand for unquestioning loyalty to his business judgement silenced relevant and sound criticism. Freddie believed that he had an open and frank relationship with his colleagues. He was quite unaware of the perfectly understandable reticence on their part to question his judgement once the decision had been made.

He had demanded a degree of loyalty from them, quite subconsciously, which they were willing to give because the risk was not theirs. This brought an air of unreality to the boardroom and distanced the entrepreneur from what had previously been a closely knit team of colleagues.

Chastened by the experience of the boatyard and an accidental report of the effect the venture had had on the confidence of his colleagues, Freddie decided to put the record straight. He sought an independent and totally frank assessment of the business venture and made sure that the findings were circulated to his colleagues. In discussing these findings with them he both castigated them for what he saw as their 'conspiracy of silence' and was self-critical of his assumption of their loyalty towards him. The accusation that the management team had conspired against him was clearly unfair but, once out in the open, revealed to Freddie the true nature of his dominant relationship over them and what needed to be done to restore or open frank communication in future. The team spirit was re-established and the danger of another failure considerably reduced.

This example deals with a major business venture. The entrepreneur's demand for loyalty is often also evident when small issues are involved. He expects people to see his point of view in relatively trivial matters and his subordinates may opt for a quiet life rather than run the risk of a damaging confrontation. Once in the habit of exerting a powerful influence in small issues the executive can find himself taking a similar approach to more weighty matters. This is a slippery slope both for the entrepreneur himself and the individual reporting to him: all successful businessmen need sounding boards for their ideas and a strong and well-informed management team is the best place to start. If the entrepreneur has got into the habit of denying free debate and expecting unquestioning loyalty, he will considerably weaken his own capability to succeed.

An uncertain temper

It has been regularly observed that entrepreneurs are more likely to be prone to rapid mood changes than their colleagues in more conventional walks of life. It seems that a dominant ambition and a strong driving force to achieve a clearly visualised personal goal lead directly to impatience in the face of obstacles or inefficiencies. Some successful entrepreneurs have been described as 'having a beguiling mixture of endless charm and a capacity for unbridled tyranny'. They are more often optimistic and extroverted than pessimistic and introverted. To be successful they need sufficient self-control to present these positive qualities to those on whose judgements they rely. However, this does not always reflect the way in which they behave in private towards those who rely on them. For example, the cheerful, outgoing and caring individual known and loved by his customers, financiers and fellow share-holders may be seen in a totally different light by his staff and suppliers. He may be intolerant, vindictive and unreasonable without this being in any way apparent outside the business. Inevitably, these personality traits leak out into the wider business community, where several examples can be found of highly successful entrepreneurs enjoying this 'Jekyll and Hyde' reputation for their external image and internal behaviour.

In some ways, this double-sided style is acceptable so long as it is consistent and people know what to expect. More worrying are those entrepreneurs whose mood changes have a deeply unsettling effect on their colleagues. Another example drawn from real life will serve to illustrate this problem.

Angus Beaver, the founder and principal shareholder in a high-tech company, has a group of senior colleagues who are devoted to him and to the business. He has always shown a caring attitude towards them as individuals and their work within the company. However, as the business moves from a stage when survival is the most important issue to relative stability and success, his real temperament starts to emerge. It becomes clear that he is insecure in his ability to drive the business further forward and consequently looks for flattery and reassurance from his colleagues. Having received it, however, he becomes suspicious of the motives of the individual concerned and reacts harshly. Those who do not fall prey to this find themselves being dealt with rationally and irrationally in turn. Public applause is followed by private criticism, communicated indirectly through another colleague. The team becomes deeply conscious of, as one of them puts it, 'walking on an organisational quicksand'. Angus's incon-sistency in dealing with his colleagues, caused by his own insecurity, is at the root of the problem. Their own confidence in him rapidly declines despite the clear evidence of the continued success of the business. Angus strives ever harder to gain the reassurance he needs but consistently fails. Ultimately, a confrontation occurs and the team desert their erstwhile leader.

It is a well-accepted management maxim that a consistently poor style is much to be preferred to one which is inconsistently good or bad. This applies even more strongly to the entrepreneur, since his relationships are built around much less conventional and hierarchical assumptions. An uncertain temper is usually a form of entrepreneurial self-indulgence, and the entrepreneur only gets away with it because of the compliance of colleagues and associates. High quality managers rarely tolerate this behaviour in their bosses nor permit it in themselves. This sometimes explains why those managers supporting entrepreneurs are so often of such uninspiring quality.

Unreliable leadership

There are many illustrations of leaders being unreliable, sometimes even misleading their subordinates to the extent that the team is wholly unprepared for the action in which they become engaged. The leader can cause confusion by rapid changes in strategy or tactics or in the distribution of roles to the members of his team. He can abandon his subordinates in the thick of the fray or fail to make crucial decisions when changes in direction are called for. Most of all, he can lose the confidence of those around him so that morale becomes irretrievably low.

Entrepreneurs are prone to any or all of these failings in precisely the same way as other business managers. The problem of identifying when and to what extent the failings occur, however, is much greater in the entrepreneurial environment since there is often little precedent to guide those involved and no rulebook to indicate normal procedures. By its very nature, entrepreneurialism is about innovation and risk-taking. In large companies 'intrapreneurialism' is a surrogate for the process which happens in less structured environments. In a large company, however, there are frameworks within which the entrepreneurial process is encouraged and monitored. The individuals involved have certain expectations of the way in which plans and decisions are likely to be communicated and progress measured. The entrepreneur may, of course, already have precedents with earlier ventures on which his subordinates can call; he may have such an organised and distinctive style that any failings in leadership on his part are quickly identified and rectified. In many cases, however, this will not be possible and problems and potential failure could follow. Let us look at an example of this problem.

William Daring is the promoter of a new venture involving the manufacture and sale of a novel form of electric pump. Well versed in the background of the industry and the relevant technology, he brings together an able team of managers and raises the necessary funds to set the venture in motion. Initial indications are promising and the market take-off of the new product gives William and his colleagues cause for satisfaction. Then one Friday night William departs unexpectedly on an overseas trip and leaves no forwarding address with his secretary. His colleagues are mystified and become alarmed when, on the following Monday William's secretary circulates a letter from an American firm of lawyers claiming that the new product is in breach of a worldwide patent. The letter goes on to threaten the company with an injunction demanding that they should cease production forthwith. In the absence of William, the management team consult their lawyers and manage to stave off the problem for three weeks, when a meeting is arranged between the American company and their lawyers and the UK team. Desperate attempts to reach William fail but calm is restored when he returns to the office a week later.

He confirms that the action taken by his team was absolutely correct but also announces that he has to visit a major customer on the day of the crucial meeting with the Americans. Nothing will persuade him to change his plans and the management team is left to negotiate a settlement in his absence. They do their best on the day but can only achieve a royalty agreement which makes a considerable dent in the firm's profits. On his return, William is deeply dissatisfied with the arrangement and attempts to recover lost ground. The die has already been cast, however, and he has to reconcile himself to a much less prosperous future than he would otherwise have expected.

His colleagues are mystified and disappointed by his

apparent lack of sensitivity to the importance of this issue. They suspect that he knew about the letter before leaving on his first trip and intentionally left them to resolve this particular crisis without his help and support. Whether true or not, the feelings deeply affect their confidence in William's judgement. He has failed them as a leader at a critical moment in the development of the company and perhaps through less than honourable motives. It took a long time for the team to recover from this apparent lapse in his otherwise energetic and effective leadership.

Those who set out to be successful entrepreneurs seldom, if ever, envisage that they may become victims of the Napoleon factor. They take on themselves, however, a significant responsibility to behave in a straightforward, consistent and effective way in their dealings with the people around them. They can be forgiven many shortcomings in terms of temper and attitude, but an insensitivity to wise counsel and an overweening confidence in their own judgement can be harbingers of problems ahead.

An impossible partner?

Much of our investigation so far has been concerned with the entrepreneur as the solo-player – the individualist who pursues his own innovatory goals with energy and enthusiasm. But sometimes entrepreneurs appear to operate in pairs or groups. Are these genuine team efforts?

Practical experience suggests that entrepreneurs are essentially dominant individuals and therefore any relationship between an entrepreneur and a 'partner' is likely to be on a footing of the second individual being in some way subordinate to the first. Genuine equality may, of course, appear to be present to the casual observer – many successful trading empires have been founded by siblings, who show complementary mental attitudes or skills. One may be a more active risk-taker and one more conservative, while an outgoing personality may be matched by a more introverted one. They appear to take their decisions jointly and one will always consult the other.

In truth, harmonious partnerships are often not what they appear. Close relationships of this nature, particularly when innovation is involved, are seldom straightforward. The reason for the partners' coming together in the first place and the experiences they have shared both influence the way in which their mutual arrangement works. It may be driven by a sense of mutual benefit – the classic equation of two plus two making five, but whatever the age or relative status of the individuals, one or other always has the final word; successful entrepreneurial partnerships will always contain one individual whose judgement overrides the other when doubt arises (although which one of the two this is can, and sometimes does, change over time without any apparent loss of common momentum). Discovering which of the partners makes the decisions is vital if you are doing business with them.

If the entrepreneurial duo consists of brothers or sisters or father and son, similarity of temperament often proves a disadvantage rather than an advantage in terms of entrepreneurial drive. There can be no hard and fast rules but entrepreneurs have a considerable need for someone close to them 'off whom sparks can be struck'. If the near relation is too much like the entrepreneur, the process is confirmatory of his judgements rather than challenging.

A good entrepreneurial partnership consists of a dominant individual and a subordinate with complementary but strongly held views. The element of respect for the other's judgement must feature large in such arrangements if they are to be permanent. Entrepreneurs are distrustful and dismissive of others' talents, hence the rarity of such partnerships. This is not to say that successful partnerships (husbands and wives are a good example) cannot do very well in finding and developing businesses. However, it is the degree of entrepreneurial challenge confronting the individuals which is the touchstone for success. For example, taking a lease on a corner shop and establishing a successful post office is an admirable enterprise for a married couple and many important decisions are doubtless involved. However, it is not comparable in scale of difficulty with another couple inventing, manufacturing and marketing a brand new product.

Few are privileged to hear the private conversations between the individuals involved in a genuinely creative and successful entrepreneurial partnership. Much will depend on the temperament, education and cultural background of the participants. However, it seems likely that planning, decision-taking and trouble-shooting involve intense feelings and strong commitment vividly and energetically expressed. The creative genius of Gilbert and Sullivan resulted from an explosive personal relationship, and Messrs Rolls and Royce did not enjoy a perennially harmonious working relationship.

The genuine entrepreneurial partner is a rare individual and undoubtedly needs exceptional qualities or strength of character, persistence and resilience. It is perhaps an accident of fate that brings such teams together and once formed they can be remarkably successful. The 'love/hate' relationship seems a common factor but an essential one for them to work well.

Follow my leader

Much more common than the entrepreneurial partner is the trusted lieutenant who is close to the entrepreneur but does not share in the final decision-taking process. Many highly successful businessmen have acquired such individuals in the course of their business progress. They can have almost any background, qualifications or set of personal attributes. The one common characteristic is that they support the entrepreneur (with total loyalty), aid and abet his activities and perform whatever is asked of them, however trivial. The analogy used by some to describe such people is that of the devoted wife always available to do her husband's bidding. This seems a little unfair on most wives in these emancipated days and a more apt comparison might be with Jeeves or Figaro, but without the element of manipulation attributed to these two famous servants.

Such trusty lieutenants are often treated outrageously and inconsistently by the entrepreneur. Abuse, sarcasm, ill-will and unreasonableness are commonplace in the case of some of the more extravagant and unpredictable entrepreneurs. The ability to tolerate and bounce back from such insensitive and unfair treatment is much admired by those less closely involved. It does raise the question, however, of why such individuals suffer these indignities rather than move elsewhere.

The answer appears to lie in the fascination which men of action and decision hold for many people. The charisma often associated with successful entrepreneurs is partly the self-confidence of the dominant individual and partly the command over people which money and power bring. This has a curious fascination for some people and can strongly influence the behaviour of otherwise mature individuals.

Many people could not, and would not, tolerate the treatment meted out to these lieutenants. They, in turn, probably would not want to change their lot with anyone else and indeed they often assume positions of considerable power and influence themselves when the entrepreneur becomes more remote from his business operations. Perhaps they are following a more subtle course than most would credit them with!

A team of heroes

Many of the most vaunted corporate entrepreneurs have built their personal reputations on closely organised teams of individuals. It is a characteristic of many high technology industries that innovation is only possible as a team enterprise and the various technical and managerial skills needed to bring a major project to fruition are the province of highly motivated and expert individuals. The team can indeed be heroic in an entrepreneurial sense. However, every such team needs, and has always needed, someone who is its leader. As discussed earlier, entrepreneurs in a large corporate environment have a different role and behave in a different way from those operating outside that system. Their skills are more likely to emphasise planning, team-building and motivation than individual innovation and risk-taking. In economic terms they are highly valuable to the country and in some senses are more influential in business development than the solo-player. By their very rarity, the individuals involved often rise rapidly to positions of great prominence and corporate seniority. There is no doubt that a blending of the attitudes and skills of the individual entrepreneur and the organisational aptitude of his corporate colleague offers a remarkably effective team combination which sadly is seldom seen in practice.

Large corporations often seek to grow by acquiring smaller or entrepreneurial companies. This is frequently the case in high technology industries in which technical breakthroughs are regularly made in small companies. The acquirer usually attempts to channel the vigorous enterprise of the owner of the small company to their mutual benefit. It seldom if ever works. The seller generally works out a contract 'earn out' period before moving on, probably to set up another small business. The critical factor is usually the smothering effect of corporate bureaucracy which ultimately deters the free thinking and decision-taking of the individual who has previously been his own boss. Corporate entrepreneurialism thrives in a few large corporations because the people involved understand and know how to play the corporate game; self-made men seldom have the time or inclination to learn the rules.

Living with a whirlwind

Sometimes, one comes across a director of a successful growing business who respects and is respected by the owner. He has done well in his role in the entrepreneur's team and managed to blend professionalism and enterprise. What is the secret?

The first rule is not to attempt to maintain either the entrepreneur's pace of work (which is usually exhausting to most people) or to keep abreast of his kaleidoscopic range of interests and activities. The director needs to have a strong sense of his personal role and identity and to act wholly consistently within it. For example, if the person concerned deals with finance, then he must understand and follow his own judgement with regard to the entrepreneur's financial affairs. He must have a consistent attitude towards risk-taking, financial probity and stewardship and the disciplines needed in the organisation and management of an effective company. These attitudes will undoubtedly bring him from time to time into conflict with the entrepreneur. He may be the butt of the latter's sense of frustration or have his loyalty questioned, but being true to his own beliefs and standards will ultimately be the most powerful contribution he can make to the team effort. Undoubtedly, the director concerned must have a thick skin, not be too easily put off by apparently eccentric behaviour, or lose confidence if his boss fails to observe the niceties of a conventional organisation. Successful entrepreneurs ultimately respect strong-minded colleagues and do not expect their subordinates either to ape their own behaviour or be yes-men. The experience of working with a successful entrepreneur is a great test of character and will for many younger managers; there is an almost irresistible temptation to become a carbon copy of the boss. It is amusing and somewhat sad to visit an entrepreneurially led company to find directors and managers alike using language and gestures which directly echo those of the dominant entrepreneur involved.

Most of all, people working for entrepreneurs need a very clear view of what they can contribute to the overall success of the enterprise. When ventures are first being set up, roles may be very confused but the end objective is very clear; the team spirit which encourages everyone to get involved in any menial task is both exhilarating and effective. As entrepreneurial enterprises grow, roles become clearer but the end objective becomes less apparent. This is a result of the impatience which entrepreneurs sometimes have with conventional management structures and decision-taking mechanisms. Thus the finance director quoted earlier may be asked to play a variety of roles depending on the immediate priorities of his boss. At one moment the operation of the petty cash control system may be under close scrutiny and at the next he may have to explain the company's long-term funding strategy in layman's terms. It is this very variety which many find the most appealing thing about working so close to the whirlwind. A calm head and a good sense of humour are also invaluable personal characteristics for those who want to make a long-term career in such people's company!

24 hours a day

Many successful entrepreneurs take pride in their unwillingness to take holidays. 'One day off in the last five years' was the boast of the owner of a successful hotel chain and an equally common expression is that 'my work is my hobby' – which to the uninitiated is either mysterious or enviable or both.

In a guide to entrepreneurial behaviour published by the International Labour Office in the mid-1970s the reader was encouraged to rise one hour earlier than usual each day as part of the regime of learning to be an entrepreneur. An extra hour a day hardly seems to match up to the extraordinary working day claimed by many self-made men. Undoubtedly, long hours and reluctantly taken holidays are a hallmark of the dedicated entrepreneur. Neglected wives and girlfriends may well use the disparaging term 'workaholic' to describe this demonic pursuit of business. The interesting question is, what is the 'work' involved and how does it compare with that done by people in more conventional jobs?

In an earlier chapter it was argued that the entrepreneur continually creates a very clear vision of the world as he wishes to see and influence it. The vision may be of every teenager wearing his brand of socks or of his commanding the most prestigious and profitable firm of advertising agents. If he is a dealer his vision is that of the successful transaction and the profits which will flow from it.

The entrepreneur's 'work' is therefore the process of bringing his vision to a reality. This process is rather like the Chinese juggler spinning a series of plates on bamboo canes. As a new plate is set spinning the juggler must return to those started earlier to keep up their momentum. The action becomes frenetic as more plates are spun and the danger of one or more falling from its pole increases. Like the Chinese juggler, the entrepreneur sees the end state of all the plates spinning as his personal vision. His energies are spent on keeping all the components working towards that common end.

The equivalent to the spinning plates in the entrepreneur's life is the attitude and decisions of those on whom he relies to carry out his plans. Research has shown that influential individuals spend between 70 and 80 per cent of their working days in conversation with others either face to face or on the telephone. These conversations are as much to do with information-gathering and persuading as with decision-taking. The entrepreneur is clearly at the centre of the decision-taking function but the process itself is often very swift. The ability to see the required decision in the context of the long-term plan is frequently exclusively that of the entrepreneur rather than of those around him. This gives him a considerable advantage in the speed and clarity of his decision-taking.

The entrepreneur's working day typically includes some strenuous physical activity even if it is restricted to a gallop around the shop floor or a chase across the tarmac to the private jet. Spare moments are spent in reading what is often a wide and ill-assorted selection of newspapers and magazines (entrepreneurs are seldom bookish) and some time in private and quiet reflection. Habits of writing or dictating letters or memoranda vary considerably but as a general rule entrepreneurs prefer to have three or four phones in the office, with a portable phone, and leave it to others to prepare anything beyond a short and crisp directive.

The characteristic energy charge which such individuals bring to their daily work is often accompanied by a low boredom threshold and a desire for variety of company and topics. This can be deceptive since the art of winning support and influencing people often demands care and patience and single-minded concentration.

This mixture of activity involves little that is routine and much that contributes to the self-generated excitement of the risk-taker. The lack of structure in itself clearly offers a sense of satisfaction to the entrepreneur. More importantly, he almost certainly feels that nothing outside his sphere of work has any comparable significance. The self-centred 'universe' which is so extraordinarily real to the entrepreneur often represents a curiously unbalanced view of life as seen by the independent observer. Work becomes a passion and pervades the individual's life, often to the exclusion of all other significant interests. Even though the entrepreneur may become known as a leading collector or philanthropist it often seems that this is no more than a diversion from what really matters – business!

Many successful men appear to find it very difficult to enjoy the wealth which they have worked so hard to earn. Brief excursions on the luxury yacht or to the hideaway on an exotic island are interrupted by frequent, and perhaps solicited, business calls. The grim determination of a relaxing entrepreneur intent on enjoying himself, come what may, is alarming and dispiriting to behold. The excitement in his life, born of his business interests, acts as a powerful motivator and potential narcotic. He is unhappy and impatient whenever the stimulus is removed.

A real life example is the case of a property tycoon whose career started in his teens when he worked as a negotiator for an estate agent. Spotting the potential of an undervalued property he persuaded a wealthy car dealer to buy the derelict building for which he then obtained planning consent. This original deal led to more joint venture initiatives and in due course to his forming his own company. He travelled the length and breadth of the country in search of sites with potential, working evenings and weekends, bank holidays and even on Christmas Day. Soon his business had grown to the size at which he could afford to recruit professional staff, who had the skill and experience to relieve him of much of the burden of site visits, negotiations with vendors and money-raising forays to the bank. Rather than reduce his workload or change his style of operation, he allowed his personal workload actually to increase. His pattern of supervising every detail meant that, as the company grew, he had even more to oversee. An obvious consequence of this process was that he suffered from a build-up of mental and physical exhaustion which resulted in a breakdown from which he never fully recovered. He agreed that the cause had been totally illogical; he went on to admit that his lifestyle, as the company had grown, had become less agreeable than when he was only accountable to himself.

The commitment to his private world was nonetheless so total that he was willing to put his health at risk. Like many successful men, he suffered from the problems of 'boundary vision' in the form of an inability to see his own enterprise in the context of the wider world.

It has been argued that a period of such total commitment is essential to the process of building a successful business. In time the individual emerges from this stage with a more balanced view of his own role and that of the organisation he has built.

Money and power

All the available research shows that, in the early stages of entrepreneurial development at least, it is the drive to become rich which is the prime motivator. The 1988 survey of British entrepreneurs demonstrated that they are drawn from a wide variety of cultural and domestic backgrounds. It would certainly be untrue to assume that the entrepreneur always springs from a background of deprivation and is motivated to catch up with his more affluent colleagues. Many of the most successful have either inherited wealth or married into money and have used this as the lever for the development of a greater fortune. Whether the pursuit of wealth is seen as an end in itself or simply as the means of accumulating more is something of a puzzle. If the premise that the entrepreneur is particularly conscious of the insecurity of his position is correct then the urge to accumulate wealth could be explained in terms of that factor alone. The need for financial security is satisfied at a relatively modest level for most people, however the entrepreneur drives onward with an apparently insatiable desire to accumulate yet more.

The paradox of piling increasing riches on wealth already gained is that it appears to have less and less influence over the entrepreneur's behaviour. Indeed, there comes a point at which the financial factor in any business equation is more meaningful to the entrepreneur in relative than in absolute terms. Thus the international trading magnate with a personal wealth of, say, £500 million is less interested in the actual cost of mounting a predatory bid on another company than in the rate of profit or capital growth he can anticipate on the deal relative to his other activities. The financial motive then becomes more refined and academic in its impact on the entrepreneur's behaviour, although the judgements he makes may remain fairly subjective and crude.

The phases of the development of this financial motivation can be characterised as follows:

- conspicuous spending;
- fortune-building; and
- aestheticism.

Conspicuous spending

The nascent entrepreneur is probably motivated as much by the things which money can buy as by the leverage it gives over the growth of the business. The degree of conspicuousness will, of course, depend very much on the temperament of the individual. It may be overt and flashy or subtle and understated. It is almost always there, however, as a tangible demonstration that the individual has 'made it'. Houses, cars, luxury holidays, furniture, pictures or other *objets d'art* are usually the sign of the 'new' rich. Simply to have them is not sufficient, of course: they must be advertised to and recognised by the entrepreneur's peer group. This rather crude exhibitionism is found neither universally nor consistently. However, it is sufficiently common to be regarded as a distinctive feature which, in some cases, remains unchanged throughout the entrepreneur's career. For most, the lifestyle satisfactions which come from newly acquired wealth start to fall into a pattern which needs no further priming by new spending and the motivating force changes. The entrepreneur then finds himself in the fortune-building phase.

Fortune-building

In this phase, the entrepreneur becomes deeply aware of his own financial progress and achievement and is often very cautious and careful in its management. For many, this phase becomes a life-long preoccupation and there are thousands of family businesses in which the original founder has successfully handed down a substantial fortune as a consequence of prudent financial management.

The financial motive remains as strong as ever but the result of his activities are handled with discretion and perhaps even secrecy. Entrepreneurs do not have to be reclusive to disguise the range and nature of their interests from the casual observer. For example, local gossip in a market town may attribute involvement in many ventures to a successful businessman who, in fact, has no part in them at all. The veil which the entrepreneur can draw over his affairs is usually penetrated by few other than his accountant and the tax inspector. This frequently works to his advantage in enabling him to create a reputation of success on the one hand and to disguise his failures on the other.

For most, the fortune-building stage starts when, perhaps, the individual's personal wealth exceeds £1 million and may continue to levels well in excess of £100 million. Above these figures, however, the third phase – aestheticism – starts to appear.

Aestheticism
With a substantial and secure fortune behind him, the active entrepreneur starts to attach a more symbolic meaning to wealth and the motivation of money than in the previous phases. Under all reasonable analysis the fortune at his disposal, unless it is precariously invested in one particular enterprise, gives him and his kin whatever security and lifestyle they might reasonably need for the foreseeable future. The basic appetites for these have long since been satisfied. The drive for further wealth accumulation continues, and even accelerates, because it is the process of entrepreneurship and the symbolic measurement of its success in financial terms which is more appealing than the actual money itself. Although not truly aesthetic, the financial sophistication and manipulative skills of the heavyweight operator often have a clinical objectivity which comes close to this epithet. This style of thinking is perhaps most evident in those who act as 'traders' under our earlier classification of entrepreneurial types. Buying and selling companies, forming new and aggressive liaisons, breaking up enterprises and dealing with governments are all grist to the mill at this most visible and high level of entrepreneurialism. The transactions involved are often highly complex and structured in very sophisticated ways. The financial ingredients are dominant and social, cultural and personal interests are frequently the least significant. The creation, planning and execution of these types of deal often have a stark simplicity with the financial consequence as their only 'reality'.

At this stage the entrepreneur becomes a game-player with the financial stakes being no more real than the plastic chips at the roulette table. The drive to accumulate more is no less remorseless, but the emphasis is on winning rather than on the number of chips themselves.

The urge for power

Money can clearly bring power to the entrepreneur in terms of commanding the world about him. At its simplest level, the successful man's ability to live more luxuriously, drive faster cars, command more attention from tailors and head waiters is proof positive to him that he stands above the common man. This simple aspect of entrepreneurial power becomes more complex as the individual's influence itself grows. The strongest element is probably his power over people. Successful entrepreneurs often claim disinterest in this aspect and a benign approach to those who work for them. Both assertions should be treated with some suspicion.

The *bonhomie* of the workplace between the owner of the business and his shop-floor employee often disguises the mutual recognition of the boss's power to decide his subordinates' future in the business. There is nothing inherently wrong in this relationship, but its presentation as something different from what it actually is can cause some disquiet. If the entrepreneur behaves consistently and fairly to his colleagues he will earn their confidence and respect. The very nature of the entrepreneurial activity, however, often demands a ruthlessness in dealing with people which many find distasteful. From the viewpoint of the entrepreneur, people are frequently no more than one element in a complex equation. Further, they are an element without significant individuality and their prime function is to facilitate the operation of the other parts.

Some entrepreneurs seem to delight in demonstrating their power over their subordinates through, for example, embarrassing or belittling them in front of their colleagues or demanding menial services of senior individuals. An entrepreneur rampant at a board meeting can be a frightening sight. His power over the destiny of his colleagues is sometimes so great that what elsewhere would be considered outrageous behaviour is accepted as being tolerable. Zoologists might suggest that the pack leader is doing no more than demonstrate his dominance over those who might challenge his position. This may be so, but the curious fact is that the remarkable powers of persuasion and not infrequent mood changes of entrepreneurs often enable them to retain the loyalty of their colleagues which might otherwise be lost through these demonstrations of authority.

The second power arena is that which the entrepreneur has over organisations external to the enterprise itself. Typically, the successful entrepreneur finds that he can directly or indirectly influence the destiny of, for example, a supplier organisation. Suppliers and customers often prosper together but the supplier's problem is frequently that of over-dependence on his principal customer. This can put considerable potential for powerful manipulation in the hands of the customer. Equally, the third party could be a trade association, a community or a local political party. Whatever the dimensions of the external body, the successful entrepreneur can often exercise a powerful influence over their judgements and decisions. This power of patronage is a strong motivating force which the entrepreneur can put to good (or bad) use.

The motive for exercising power and influence in such situations can sometimes be traced back to the entrepreneur's underlying wish to be recognised. Despite being critical of established institutions, entrepreneurs are often more than ready to accept their accolades. Thus chairmanships of charitable bodies, boards of school governors or health authorities or honorary degrees or other titles prove remarkably agreeable to those who have spent their earlier careers castigating the establishment! The reality of power and the extent of overt recognition of personal achievement become blurred in these more mature stages of the entrepreneurs' careers. Many businessmen have much more real power over people when operating in private than when holding some eminent public office.

Lastly, there is the power which the entrepreneur wields over the development of products, markets, and consumer behaviour. To be able to say that you have changed the course of economic development through the introduction of a new material or product is to recognise a special form of power. The urge to innovate which we discussed earlier links directly to the satisfactions to be gained from this source. The mixture of these three essential ingredients will vary from one individual to another. In the last analysis, however, a combination of money and power proves irresistible.

Family man

As dominant individualists it is hardly surprising that many entrepreneurs prove difficult marriage partners. There are examples of highly successful husband-and-wife entrepreneurial partnerships, which suggest that a like-minded attitude towards the excitement of wealth creation has a strong mutual attraction. In public, such marital partnerships often present a powerful and persuasive image. As argued earlier, however, all entrepreneurial duos contain one individual whose judgement and influence is significantly more powerful than the other. The same is invariably true of the more private lives of married couples, whether or not they work together in business. In many areas of business, particularly those involving services, a husband-and-wife team is an attractive promotional proposition. In reality, the one who is the 'junior' partner is likely to have a fairly stressful existence unless well tuned to the particular role he or she is asked to play.

That role can range from keeping a high public profile to extreme domestic privacy. In the former case, the male entrepreneur often seems to want to share his success in public with his wife; in the latter, he clearly separates his more visible business activities from his private life. Thus his wife may become as well known as the husband himself. For example, Sir Bernard Docker, a very successful engineering magnate of the 1950s, ultimately became less well known than his flamboyant wife, Lady Dorothy Docker. There could be no question that Sir Bernard was the successful entrepreneur, nor perhaps any doubt that he got as much pleasure from the reputation earned by his wife as he did by his business ventures. The majority of entrepreneurs are conversely more concerned with keeping their wives out of the public arena than thrusting them into it.

Private lives

In private, entrepreneurs' wives (or husbands) have to deal with individuals whose temperament and approach to life can make them extremely difficult to live with. An entrepreneur's wife confided that her husband was:

- more interested in anything connected with the business than with his wife and family;
- impatient and short-tempered, sometimes treating the domestic situation as a simple extension of the challenges of business;

- unable to relax and enjoy fully leisure activities with the family; and
- of variable moods, depending on the pressures of his business life.

This may seem rather an extreme case, but the high emotional charge which is associated with the wealth-creation process must often leave the entrepreneur drained of energy and enthusiasm for more mundane interests. Experience suggests that such people recognise at an early stage in their careers that they will benefit from marriage. A supportive wife can be a crucial factor in making difficult decisions, despite the fact that the responsibility of the family man is much greater than that of the bachelor. Entrepreneurs therefore tend to marry at a relatively early age and at the beginning of their careers. In consequence, they encounter the problems of developing their own personality and lifestyle at a pace and in a direction which may not be matched by that of their partners. Neither may originally envisage the nature of the demands to be made on each other. The day-to-day pressures on the relationship, particularly when the personal and financial risks involved are extreme, can be enormous. It is these pressures most evident in private life that can cause the spectacular marriage break-ups which are often associated with the successful businessman.

An argument can be made for the case that entrepreneurs are essentially loners and that any form of permanent personal relationship runs counter to their nature. This loneliness itself stems from a feeling of being at odds with the world and the constant desire to demonstrate individual success. While there is some truth to be found in this analysis, it denies the obvious effects of the passage of time. Older and more experienced people inevitably become more circumspect in their behaviour and often see changing values in their personal relationships. Thus the importance of the family and, in particular, the role of the entrepreneur's children, gain more importance as his own career moves through middle age. The image of the contented self-made man, benevolent to those around him, handing on his business to a grateful younger generation, is as far-fetched as that of the miserly recluse hoarding his millions. As a general rule, however, it seems that entrepreneurs become relatively easier to live with as they get older and experience tempers the fiery impatience of youth.

Keeping it in the family

The question of nepotism is one which deeply affects many who have succeeded in building a successful enterprise. It seems to them almost an affront that a younger generation should have any reservation about taking on the stewardship of the family future. For the entrepreneur, it is the ultimate disappointment if that generation simply wishes to enjoy the financial spoils without accepting some mantle of continued business involvement.

When asked the question, 'What is all this exhausting expenditure of time and effort for?', the reply will frequently be 'for the benefit of my family'. The truth is that the family are seldom consulted and the entrepreneur makes assumptions about their interest which frequently prove unfounded.

Public markets for shares have grown enormously in recent years and flotation is no longer a privilege accorded only to large and established companies. Business founders increasingly see the benefit of having their equity interest reflected in marketable securities. In theory at least they can easily sell their shares, if they so wish, at a price which considerably exceeds that available to a private company. There are, of course, some disadvantages. A public company is very much in the public eye and the principal shareholder may find himself more accountable to the market-place and to the commentary (whether complimentary or critical) of financial analysts. A quoted company is also more vulnerable to unwelcome and predatory takeovers. Nonetheless, many family enterprises which would, in earlier times, have remained just that lose their unique entrepreneurial identity within a single generation.

A dynastic approach to business is much less common now than it was 50 or 100 years ago. Many entrepreneurs are selling their businesses in early middle age and perhaps going on to found another fortune, having provided for their family from the first. The reason is that there is no longer an automatic succession of children to family businesses. This is partly because nowadays children are both better educated and have a wider range of personal choice. It is also because the social assumptions surrounding businesses have themselves changed and a recognition of the need for professional management is more widespread. Thus the old adage 'from rags to riches and back again in three generations' is seen by many as very true. The entrepreneurial wizardry of one generation is seldom if ever perpetuated by the next. Even entrepreneurs themselves, albeit reluctantly, now recognise that the handing on of power is seldom either desirable or practical.

The reality is that the fortune has to be handed down to a new generation of owners who are likely to be supported by professional managers and advisers rather than being directly involved in the wealth-creation process themselves. The entrepreneur must recognise the role of his successors quite some time before he is in a position to hand over the reins. This can be a painful and difficult process for him and his immediate family. It can involve strong feelings of guilt on either side and, as a result, quite irrational and unreasonable behaviour. An entrepreneur's son might, for example, 'drop out' and take to a dissolute life rather than face up to the reality of his unwillingness to become involved in the family business. The father might fail to understand the underlying cause of his son's behaviour and, try as he might, have little influence over it until this root cause is recognised.

These problems are often further complicated by feelings of inadequacy in a particularly successful and powerful parent. The psychology is complex and needs a fair degree of thought and self-analysis on the part of the entrepreneur. This is often not the strong point of the individual concerned and a crisis occurs through lack of sensible forethought. The symptoms are often plain to see from the standpoint of the outsider but are swept to one side by the busy and successful business-builder.

Summary

The entrepreneur can easily become a prima donna in both his relationships with those who work for him and those who share his private life. Some of the characteristics of a prima donna are essential to the success of the individual; they help him to be single-minded and energetic in his approach to the challenges of his career. On the other hand, they can make him an uncomfortable and difficult colleague who would be unbearable company if it weren't for the special talents and abilities that he brings to his primary role as innovator and business-developer. He is often an unsuccessful family man, married more closely to his business than to his wife. Although middle age often brings a change in values, by then it is often too late.

Chapter 7

Summing up

Our investigation has lead us through most aspects of the life and behaviour of the entrepreneur. Much of the evidence is conflicting and the available research, such as it is, incomplete; many of the conclusions which can be drawn are inevitably controversial while others are no more than statements of the self-evident. In any event, there must be a ready and absolute recognition that we are not dealing with a comfortably classifiable species with definable characteristics and behaviour. Entrepreneurs have always sprung, and will doubtless continue to spring, from a variety of backgrounds and personal circumstances and attempts at generalisation would be dangerous. And yet powerful evidence supports the notion that certain elements of attitudes, motives and behaviour occur so frequently that a pattern is discernible.

This pattern, the 'character set' as one may call it, has been the principal focus of this book and the common thread of argument which runs through it. Many entrepreneurs surround themselves with an aura of mystique which sometimes verges on a personal mythology. As they mature and prosper they have an ever-increasing interest in its perpetuation and enhancement – it is all part of the projection of an image of themselves which they wish to impose on the world. It satisfies not only their needs but also those of others who lack the curiosity or opportunity to enquire more deeply.

This image of the entrepreneur offers us folk heroes in an age dominated by faceless corporatism, but is it accurate? Does it give a true description of the man as he really is rather than as he would like us to see him? 'No man is a hero to his valet' is an old but wise adage. In his nakedness, does the entrepreneur live up to our expectations or is there a dark side to his nature and his behaviour?

The simple answer to these questions is that entrepreneurs are exceptional individuals in whom certain common character traits are so highly accentuated (or, if you like, distorted) that they behave quite abnormally compared to the rest of us. Their economic influence is generally beneficial: they break the rules, innovate, take risks and create wealth (not least for themselves); their personal behaviour is often partial, unpredictable, unfair and destructive; their enterprise brings benefits to society at large, but their personal behaviour is likely to have a disturbing effect on their colleagues and associates. They are by turns benefactors and rebels – an admirable group of men and women with much to teach us about enterprise, and much to warn us of in terms of exaggerated personal style.

Alike or different?

By concentrating on the character set of entrepreneurs, we draw together those aspects which entrepreneurs are likely to have in common. To this extent they can be said to be 'alike'. Equally, the great diversity of activities and businesses in which they engage should be acknowledged. There seems to be no aspect of industry, commerce or services which does not throw up potential opportunities for the budding entrepreneur. Whether innovatory in the true sense of creating a new product or service or simply exploiting the application of an old one, the scope seems boundless. Nor is it limited by age, means or educational background. The 'incubator' theory suggests that some individuals need the right environment in which to develop their nascent talents. Conversely, many entrepreneurs and especially those with a strong trading instinct start their careers well before they have entered the structured world of business.

Both men and women show talent for entrepreneurialism, although the great majority of entrepreneurs to date are male – a reflection perhaps on the reality of equal opportunity rather than on the theory. Failure rates are high and many venture capitalists would give their eye teeth for the skill of invariably spotting the winners.

In all these respects, entrepreneurs are as different from one another as they are from the rest of us. They have, however, much more in common than they may readily admit to; the pattern constantly recurs. It is in recognising this and building upon it that the future of a more positive approach to entrepreneurialism can be developed.

Developing entrepreneurial capacity

The essence of a more positive approach must be to reduce the 'accidental' way in which incipient talents are brought to mature realisation. In a society geared to rewarding conformity this is no easy task. In essence it requires:

- an early recognition of relevant talents;
- a conscious commitment to creating the most propitious environment for their development; and
- a changed attitude towards failure.

In the Introduction we listed a number of 'tendencies' which single out the entrepreneur from his fellow-men. These are likely to show themselves in school, at university or in the early stages of employment. With some honourable exceptions, the institutions involved act generally to suppress or inhibit them since they are seen to be either disruptive or anti-cultural. The frustration this causes may, of course, serve to make such individuals more purposeful and act as a coarse 'filter' in selecting the more robust from their weaker brethren. It is more likely that it defers the development of nascent talent and restricts its opportunity. The argument can be made, therefore, that where the pattern is recognised the obligation of the institution should be to encourage and foster it (with all the attendant risks) rather than to suppress it.

Employers bound by conventional notions of authority and hierarchy normally find it difficult to provide the 'incubator' conditions in which potential entrepreneurs can spread their wings. Strangely enough, small, entrepreneurially led businesses are usually the worst breeding-grounds and large organisations the best. Institutionally organised firms struggle with concepts of 'intrapreneurship' but very rarely prove capable of delivering the freedom and support the individual needs. Management buy-outs which threw up 'born-again capitalists' frequently reveal an entrepreneurial capacity wholly unrecognised under more conventional management regimes. Developing an internal enterprise culture within a large firm is no easy matter. However, it *can* be done if the rewards of success (capital growth, esteem, freedom of action and so on) are recognised as realistically as the penalties of failure.

Failure is often seen as the 'tempering' by which the metal of the entrepreneur's abilities are proved. Attitudes to failure vary widely, both between those promoting ventures and those backing them. However, a more rational approach to entrepreneurialism will only be developed if:

- a more rigorous approach is adopted to recognising failure; and
- it is seen as part of a learning process.

suggesting it is something we learn

A more rigorous approach means dealing crisply and surgically with a venture when it fails rather than delaying, fudging and temporising when the inevitable is clearly unavoidable. Both entrepreneurs and backers are frequently equally guilty in this regard. Failure as part of the learning process suggests that if the basic talents are there the beneficial lessons should be emphasised rather than the loss of credibility or venture investment. The 'high risk, high returns' philosophy in the United States has much to teach more conservative and cautious Europeans.

Each of these factors offers an opportunity to increase the 'strike rate' in terms of both the number of potential entrepreneurs identified and encouraged and the business success achieved.

Golden rules for the entrepreneur

But what of the entrepreneur himself? His chosen career is lonely, fraught with risk and beset with difficulty and potential failure. He is scorned if he fails and probably disliked if he succeeds. Success itself may bring no more than a renewed urge to pursue a personal regime which is exhausting physically, mentally and emotionally. What golden rules should he follow?

Rule 1. Know yourself
The incidence of self-delusion among entrepreneurs is astonishingly high. In small doses it is not only harmless but positively beneficial; in large doses it usually leads to failure. If the entrepreneur finds understanding himself a tough process, he should turn to a reliable and frank confidant.

Rule 2. Be thorough
He should take note of the saying 'For the want of a nail the shoe was lost, for the want of a shoe the horse was lost, for the want of a horse the battle was lost.' Many brilliantly conceived entrepreneurial schemes fail through some trifling oversight. There is no one to blame but the entrepreneur himself.

Rule 3. Be consistent

However variable his temperament and attitude to people, he must try hard to act consistently. Nothing discomforts the people around the entrepreneur more than not knowing from one moment to the next how he will react to a given situation. Keeping them on their toes is one thing; destroying their ability to act effectively is another.

Rule 4. Cut your losses

It does not matter a scrap whether or not the entrepreneur is a good (or bad) loser. What matters is that he should recognise and deal with an inevitable failure before others take that initiative for him. This is not to suggest that the convinced entrepreneur should not persist in his attempts to prove that success can be achieved long after others have fallen by the wayside. It simply means that when he recognises the inevitable he should act swiftly.

Rule 5. Look for crossroads

There are crossroads at various points in an entrepreneur's career, and these are frequently overlooked at the expense of later frustration or discontent. One occurs when the first fortune is made, giving him enough money to cater for all his material needs. The second may be when choices between domestic, 'quality of life' activities and business options have to be made. The choice of developing a different, less involved management approach (or not) may be another. If crossroads are properly recognised and the choices analysed, the entrepreneur will at least be more in charge of his destiny than might otherwise be the case.

Rule 6. Be prepared to change

This is the most difficult, but probably the most crucial, of the golden rules. Progress relies on change – change in attitudes and skills, change resulting from learning from experience, change induced by the influence of friends and associates and by the example of successful peers. Success achieved too easily (or too early) can suggest a degree of infallibility which is, in truth, illusory. Entrepreneurialism is not, and can never be, about formulae or standard methods. It relies on the inspiration to take advantage of circumstances undergoing change. This requires the entrepreneur himself to change, to sharpen his skills and to build on his business achievements by constantly receiving, and if needed, reviewing his approach.

The naked entrepreneur

Stripped of the self-seeking promotion and the adulation of the gossip columns we find a workaholic dedicated to the pursuit of wealth and power. Complex in his makeup, often careless of personal relationships, he has a view of the world which is very different from the rest of us. He is in charge of his destiny, embraces extraordinary risks but in many respects acts with caution and circumspection. His enthusiasm for his career gains momentum rather than loses it as material success is achieved. Winning the competitive 'game' is more important than the financial stakes which become mere counters on the board. Meglomania waits in the wings while the world both envies and dislikes continued success. Seldom lovable but always exciting to work with, and for, entrepreneurs are mainsprings in an enterprise culture. Long may they remain so.

Bibliography

Books

Meredith, Nelson and Neck, *Practice of Entrepreneurship* (International Labour Office 1985)

Peter Drucker, *Innovation and Entrepreneurship* (Heinemann 1985)

John Chudley, *Letraset – A Lesson in Growth* (Business Books Ltd 1974)

Additionally, there are numerous popular biographies and autobiographies of individual entrepreneurs.

Research paper

Sue Birley and Liz Watson, *The British Entrepreneur 1988* (Cranfield School of Management and Arthur Young)

Articles

Howard H Stevenson and David E Gumpert 'The Heart of Entrepreneurship' (*Harvard Business Review* March–April 1985)

John G Burch, 'Profiling the Entrepreneur' (*Business Horizons* September–October 1986)

Dr Stanley Cromie, 'Motivations of Aspiring Male and Female Entrepreneurs' (*Journal of Occupational Behaviour* Vol 251–261 1987)

David Clutterbuck and Marion Devine, 'Why Start Ups Start' (*Management Today* July 1985)

Unattributed, 'What Makes an Entrepreneur?' (*Director* July 1986)

H S Cranston and Eric G Flamholtz, 'The Role of Management Development in Making the Transition from an Entrepreneurship to a Professionally Managed Organisation' (*Journal of Management Development* Vol 5 No 1 1986)

Elizabeth Chell, 'The Entrepreneurial Personality: A Few Ghosts Laid to Rest?' (*International Small Business Journal* Spring 1985)

Robert B Reich, 'Entrepreneurship Reconsidered: the Team as Hero' (*Harvard Business Review* May–June 1987)

Justin G Longenecker Jospeh A McKinney and Carlos W Moore, 'Egoism and Independence: Entrepreneurial Ethics' (*Organisation Dynamics* October 1988)

Richard Branson, 'Risk Taking' (*Journal of General Management* Vol II no 2 Winter 1985)

Manfred F R Kets de Vries, 'The Dark Side of Entrepreneurship' (*Harvard Business Review* November–December 1985)

Roger Kaplan, 'Entrepreneurship Reconsidered: The Antimanagement Bias' (*Harvard Business Review* May-June 1987)

David P Boyd and David E Gumpert 'Coping With Entrepreneurial Stress' (*Harvard Business Review* March–April 1983)

George T Solomon and Lloyd W Fernald, 'Value Profiles of Male and Female Entrepreneurs' (*International Small Business Journal* April–June 1988)

David E Gumpert and David P Boyd, 'The Loneliness of the Small-Business Owner' (*Harvard Business Review* November–December 1984)

Vesa Routamaa and Jukka Vasalainen, 'Types of Entrepreneur and Strategic Level Goal Setting' (*International Small Business Journal* Spring 1987)

Theodore D Weinshall and Lister Vickery, 'Entrepreneurs: A Balanced View of their Role in Innovation and Growth' (*European Management Journal* Winter 1987)

Arnold C Cooper and William C Dunkelberg, 'Entrepreneurship and Paths to Business' (*Strategic Management Journal* January–February 1986)

Ken G Smith Martin J Gannon, Curtis Grimm and Terence R Mitchell, 'Decision-Making Behaviour in Smaller Entrepreneurial and Larger Professionally Managed Firms' (*Journal of Business Venturing* Summer 1988)

Jeffrey G Covin and Dennis P Slevin, 'The Influence of Organisation Structure on the Utility of an Entrepreneurial Top Management Style' (*Journal of Management Studies* May 1988)

Howard H Stevenson and Carlos Jarrillo-Mossi, 'Preserving Entrepreneurship as Companies Grow' (*The Journal of Business Strategy* Summer 1986)

Glenn H Matthews, 'Run Your Business or Build an Organisation' (*Harvard Business Review* March–April 1984)

Timothy W Firnstahl, 'Letting Go' (*Harvard Business Review* September–October 1986)

Stuart Slatter, Roy Ransley and Elizabeth Woods, 'USM Chief Executives: Do They Fit the Entrepreneurial Stereotype?' (*International Small Business Journal* Vol 6 No 3)

Index